AN OPINIONATED GUIDE

BRITISH CABINS AND HIDEAWAYS

Holly Farrier

Edited by
Emmy Watts

HOXTON MINI PRESS

The Cable Hut (no.30)

Waterfall Cabin (no.31)

Aurora (no.21)

Holly Farrier (@hollyfarrierphotography) is a British photographer, whose work spans interiors, food and travel. She lives by the sea in Whitstable with her partner Dan, and travels internationally for numerous magazines, publishers and brands. There's nothing she loves more than a long weekend in a cabin, immersed in nature.

Hoxton Mini Press is a small indie publisher based in east London. We make books with a dedication to good photography, passionate writing and lovely production. When we started the company people told us 'print was dead'. That inspired us. Books are no longer about information but objects in their own right: something to collect and own and inspire.

LONG LIVE OPINION

We know that a couple of hours trawling the internet will turn up plenty of cabins and hideaways, but what you won't find online is a pithy, opinionated selection of just the very best. If you don't like our taste then you won't like these places – but if you've read this far we're pretty sure you'll love them. And these are places that you can actually stay in – they don't need to remain on your coffee table. From the Cambrian mountains to the Norfolk broads, the Cornish coast to the Scottish Highlands, we've found the most exceptional retreats, whether you want seclusion, style, luxury, natural wonder, a total detox or all of the above.

We all need the occasional escape from modern life. We spend too much time on our screens and not enough time appreciating the beauty that's within reach – and with those that are close to us. You don't have to go far to find the sanctuary you're craving; from expansive beaches to dense woodland, craggy cliff faces to rolling hills, all the cabins and hideaways in this book offer a slice of British wilderness that will leave you feeling reconnected. Reconnected to yourself, to the world around you and not just the internet.

Want more opinion?
Other *Opinionated Guides* to Britain include
British Boutique Hotels
British Family Escapes
British Cabins & Hideaways

SCOTLAND
ENGLAND
WALES
37
35
38
34
36
29
28
26
27
23
31
32
22
33
30
24
6
25
18
3
4
5
20
16
12
1
19
10
14
2
7
15
8
9
17
21
13
11

THE LOCATIONS

SOUTH EAST ENGLAND

1. Copse Cabin
2. Redwood
3. Elmley Nature Reserve
4. The Sportsman
5. Bearsted Lodge
6. Koya, Unplugged
7. Radar

SOUTH WEST ENGLAND

8. Kudhva
9. The Danish Cabin
10. Hulder Cabin
11. Lakeside Cabin
12. North Devon Hideaway
13. Bowcombe Boathouse
14. Buck's Coppice
15. Catkins Huts
16. Author's Escape
17. Firefly
18. The Tree House
19. Architect's Hut
20. Saltwater Cabin
21. Aurora

WEST MIDLANDS

22. Cynefin Retreats
23. The Bivvy
24. Fifinella Retreat
25. The Hudnalls Hideout

EAST ENGLAND

26. The Water Cabin
27. Settle

NORTH ENGLAND

28. Turf House
29. Trees at Tughall

WALES

30. The Cable Hut
31. Waterfall Cabin
32. Hergest Lee
33. Fforest Farm

SCOTLAND

34. Eagle Brae
35. Harlosh
36. The Lodge Dun Aluinn
37. Blue Hare
38. 57 Nord

THE BEST FOR...

A DIGITAL DETOX

Feeling like a slave to social media? Set yourself free with an off-grid retreat to the North Devon Hideaway (no.12), the Bivvy (no.23), Buck's Coppice (no.14) or the Architect's Hut (no.19) – all delightfully disconnected. Or, if you're dealing with a particularly severe addiction, head to one of Unplugged's (no.6) dedicated detox cabins, where you can literally lock up your phone and throw away the key (or at least hide it for the duration of your stay).

OUTDOOR ADVENTURES

Outdoorsy types will feel right at home at Eagle Brae (no.34) where adventures range from dog sledding to pony trekking, while water babies will go wild for Saltwater (no.20) and the Water Cabin (no.26) with their exciting surf and paddleboarding opportunities. Serious thrill seekers, though, should head straight to Blue Hare (no.37), where all manner of not-so-well-trodden hiking trails across the rugged Hebrides await intrepid explorers.

GOOD FOOD

Harlosh (no.35) is perfectly placed for some of Scotland's finest restaurants, while Copse Cabin (no.1) boasts an excellent on-site farm shop and cafe. The Sportsman's cabins (no.4) are handily camped out in the back garden of a Michelin-starred restaurant.

FAMILIES

Cabin life is child's play at Hergest Lee (no.32) and Fifinella Retreat (no.24), where kids slumber in cosy cubby holes. The Saltbox (no.3) in Elmley Nature Reserve comfortably accommodates adventurous little ones on a pull-out bed or hammock, while a weekend at the Turf House (no.28) is guaranteed to enchant tinies.

ROMANTIC RETREATS

With its own suspended stargazing net and wood-fired hot tub, Waterfall (no.31) feels worthy of a particularly epic love story. Likewise, Redwood's (no.2) secluded woodland setting makes it perfect for intimate getaways, while Cynefin Retreats' (no.22) idyllic cabins have been designed with couples in mind.

BIGGER GROUPS If you're seeking a mates' escape with a difference, look no further than the Danish Cabin (no.9), a spectacular off-grid retreat with its own in-house bar; or Fforest (no.33), a community resort with summer-camp vibes. Or, if it's more of a luxe feel you're after, drag the gang to Dun Aluinn (no.36), where sumptuous ensuite rooms and chef-prepared meals await.

A TOUCH OF LUXURY When you long for the remoteness of a cabin but still demand your creature comforts, head to Settle (no.27), an exceptional slow-living retreat buried in private parkland; or 57 Nord (no.38), a coastal haven with all the indulgent appeal of a high-end spa. Or why not go all out and book The Tree House (no.18), an opulent treetop sanctuary that's just the thing for special occasions.

SMALLER BUDGETS You shouldn't need to remortgage your home just so you can afford to get away from it once in a while. With their spectacular natural surroundings, the unique Kudhva pods (no.8), ramshackle Bivvy (no.23) and cosy North Devon Hideaway (no.12) are all guaranteed to make you feel like you've had a proper break, without breaking the bank.

SECLUDED STAYS Nothing says remote like Harris, the ethereal Hebridean island that's home to the spectacular Blue Hare (no.37). Or what about Waterfall (no.31), an off-grid retreat nestled deep in the Cambrian Mountains? And then there's the Danish Cabin (no.9), an intimate hideaway in a disused slate quarry that's so secluded you'll think you've journeyed to another planet.

SOMETHING DIFFERENT Ever wondered what it was like to be a Viking? The quirky Turf House (no.28) offers themed interiors and remarkably authentic experiences that will let you find out. Meanwhile, the Author's Escape (no.16) allows you to explore a slice of literary history tucked away in a writer's hut at the bottom of the garden. And there's nowhere quite like Radar (no.7), an eccentric hideaway set in an otherworldly landscape.

1

COPSE CABIN

Secluded woodland hideaway with on-site sauna

There are plenty of good reasons to book a stay in this architect-designed, tree-shrouded cabin, from its idyllic location on the edge of High Weald, an Area of Outstanding Natural Beauty, to its spectacular walk-in shower room, which boasts mesmerising views of the surrounding woodland from its full-height windows. What really sets this place apart, however, is its enticing wood-fired sauna. It might look more like a Japanese tea hut than somewhere to soothe sore muscles, but a session here will elevate your stay with its verdant views and healing properties. Wellness is the buzzword here, with Wi-Fi and TV eschewed in favour of slowing down, connecting with nature, tucking into local produce from the neighbouring farm shop and switching off completely in that spectacular sauna. We'll see you on the other side.

Catsfield, East Sussex TN33
kiphideaways.com

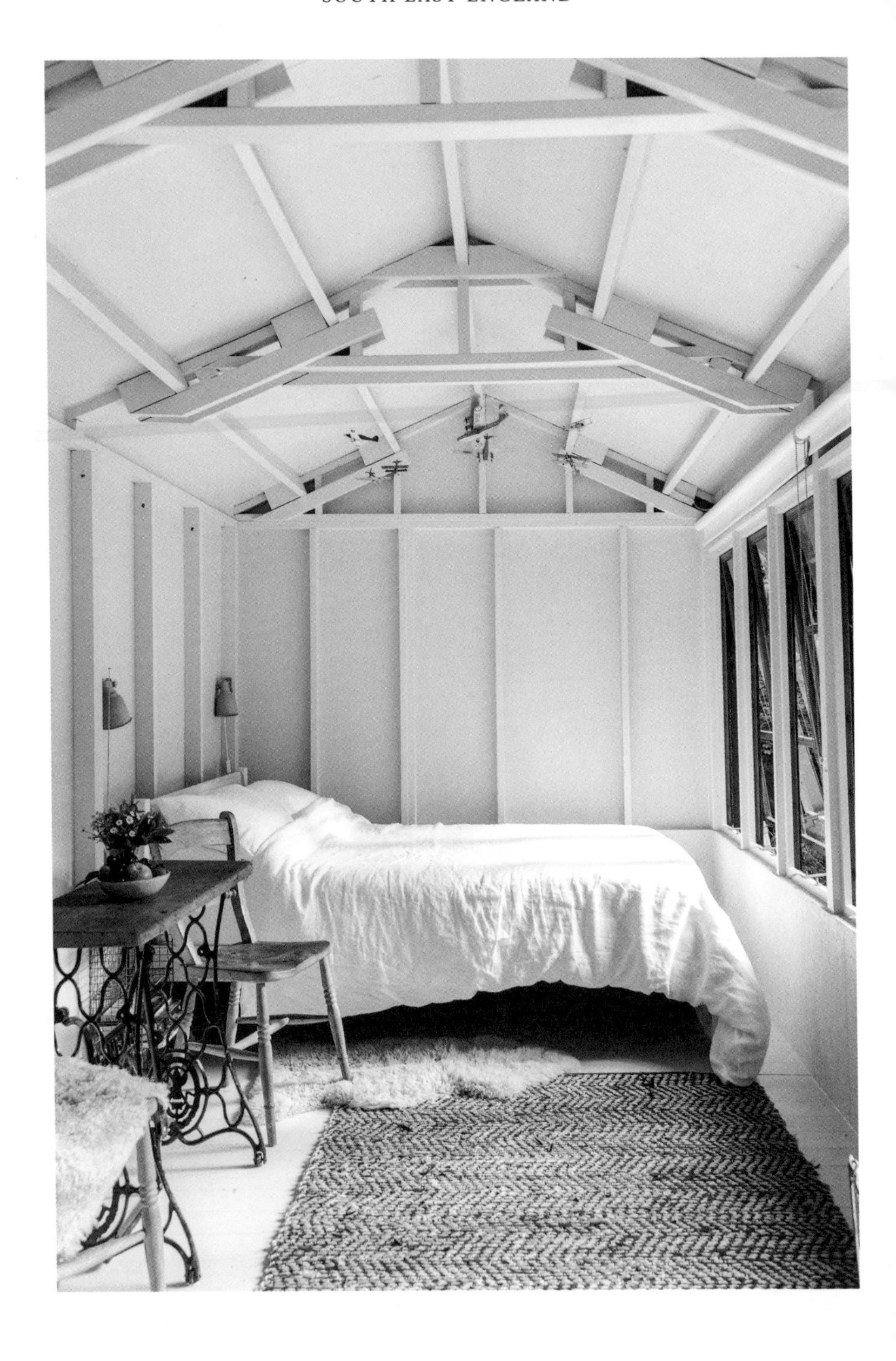

DESIGN Painted black on the outside to blend in with the shady woodland and white on the inside to create a sense of space and light, Copse feels like the archetypal cabin-in-the-woods, with cottage-cool interiors and cleverly placed windows designed to submerge you in its leafy surrounds. The bathroom extension feels particularly escapist, with floor-to-ceiling windows affording mesmerising views from the walk-in shower (and the toilet), creating the illusion that you're completely at one with nature.

FACILITIES The sauna needs to be booked ahead but will likely be a cornerstone of your stay. While there's no TV or Wi-Fi, there are more than enough games and books provided to keep you busy, and a pair of binoculars allows for some furtive wildlife watching. There's also a small kitchen that's been furnished with everything you'll need, and a delicious farm-shop breakfast is delivered each morning – usually with a slice or two of freshly baked cake for dessert.

LOCATION The cabin is located on Great Park Farm, a rural farm shop, garden centre and cafe on the edge of the ancient village of Catsfield. As well as supplying the breakfasts, the farm shop sells a variety of local produce, and being able to pick up a flat white from the adjoining cafe in the morning is a real highlight of this otherwise remote location.

NEARBY While your plan might be to hole yourself up in nature and take a break from reality during your stay, it's hard to resist the surrounding charms of East Sussex. Choose from the historic Battle Abbey, a short drive or hike away, or the seaside resorts of Hastings and Eastbourne, which are also easily reachable by car.

2

REDWOOD

Architectural eco-lodge in secluded private woodland

Perched on a leafy knoll in an Area of Outstanding Natural Beauty, this stilted minimalist hideaway wouldn't look out of place in the Hollywood Hills. Inside, there's just as much star quality, with a James Bond-style floating fireplace, full-height electrochromic panoramic windows and elegant designer furniture. But while its East Sussex setting doesn't boast quite the same concentration of film stars as California (or such reliable weather), it's even more blissfully secluded, concealed within a dense forest of rare trees, including the eponymous Giant Redwood. Ideal for romantic getaways, or even solo travellers in need of some headspace, this sustainably designed sanctuary offers a tranquil escape from reality whatever the weather, plus plenty to do on the doorstep, from coastal paths and cosy pubs to medieval citadels.

Battery Hill, Fairlight, Hastings TN35 4AL

07852 192719

kiphideaways.com

DESIGN There's a sense that every inch of Redwood has been obsessed over, from the underfloor heating to the stunning minimalist exterior and electrochromic windows – whose tint adjusts to offer privacy at night and protect animals during the day. Luxurious without being ostentatious, the lodge is stylishly furnished with a sofa and armchair from Danish designers HAY and Carl Hansen respectively, as well as a handsome kitchen with birch ply joinery and contemporary lighting throughout. Biophilically designed to immerse guests in the landscape without having a negative impact on the environment, the lodge has been sensitively constructed by local craftspeople, and manages to feel warm and welcoming despite those gargantuan windows.

FACILITIES If you fancy a slice of the great outdoors but crave your home comforts too, Redwood's comprehensive list of amenities should tick all your boxes. In addition to its open-plan living area with floating log burner, sumptuous bedroom with freestanding bath and a separate shower room, the lodge comes complete with a record player and curated vinyl, a Dyson hairdryer, locally produced toiletries, a coffee maker with compostable pods and even a Smeg hot chocolate maker with luxury Knoops hot chocolate for a decadent bedtime treat.

LOCATION Redwood is ideal for those who desire a sense of escapism without being too far from civilisation, set in ancient woodland of the High Weald but still close to towns such as Rye and St Leonards-on-Sea. The views are best enjoyed from the comfort of the expansive outdoor terrace – though the picture windows allow you to experience the surroundings without so much as lifting your head off the pillow.

NEARBY If you like having lots to do on your doorstep, Redwood will be right up your street, a short drive from the dunes of Camber Sands, the cobbled lanes of medieval Rye and quirky St Leonards-on-Sea with its vibrant Heist Street food market. Alternatively, head out on foot to absorb dramatic coastal scenery at Hastings Country Park Nature Reserve or enjoy great food and drinks at the local pub, The Cove – just a 15-minute walk away.

The cabin is set inside an ancient woodland, within the High Weald Area of Outstanding Natural Beauty.

3

ELMLEY NATURE RESERVE

Luxe cabin within a spectacular nature reserve

You've probably visited the odd nature reserve. Perhaps you've stayed in a cabin. But have you ever stayed in a cabin on a nature reserve? Elmley, a 3,300-acre wilderness on Kent's Isle of Sheppey, makes the dream a reality. The only nature reserve in the UK that permits overnight stays, Elmley has a selection of custom-made huts, luxurious tents and elegant farmhouse accommodation to choose from. A paradise for nature-loving families, the Saltbox is one of Elmley's larger cabins, with a glass wall at one end offering impressive views across far-reaching fields and marshes, as well as space to sleep two children. More than 40 species of birds breed at Elmley, which makes staying here feel like an extended avian safari, with plenty to see from the comfort of your bed and no shortage of breathtaking walks.

Elmley National Nature Reserve,
Isle of Sheppey, Kent ME12 3RW
01795 664896
elmleynaturereserve.co.uk

The only family-run National Nature Reserve in the UK, Elmley's owners aim to restore biodiversity in the area.

DESIGN The floor-to-ceiling window is an ingenious feature of Elmley's cabins, providing total immersion in your surroundings whatever the time of day or night. Trifold doors open directly onto the reserve, creating the sense of infinite space despite its small interior. Indeed, size really doesn't matter at the Saltbox, which feels defiantly luxurious with its king-size bed, small but nonetheless well-equipped kitchen and a bathroom that comes fully stocked with high-end toiletries.

FACILITIES Elmley offers seasonal breakfasts and evening dining at the on-site farmhouse. Or, if leaving your hut is just too hard, you can request locally sourced breakfast and dinner hampers to be personally delivered to your cabin. There's also a small kitchen complete with gas hob, mini oven and fridge for cooking up tasty suppers, and a cosy firepit and bistro set outside where you can enjoy the fruits of your labour. A small pull-out bed and hammock provide sleeping space for under-10s (though if you're bringing two children, at least one of them must be under six).

LOCATION Location is everything at Elmley, and there's nothing quite like waking up to those wildlife-rich views. There are several accommodation options on site, and yet there's still a pervading sense that you're completely on your own, save for the birds and the occasional hare. As one might expect of a nature reserve, there are plentiful walks at your feet, as well as well-placed bird hides for surreptitious spotting.

NEARBY This really is somewhere you could very happily hibernate in for days, but supposing the urge to explore grabs you, head to nearby Whitstable for seafood and boutiques or to Seasalter's Michelin-starred The Sportsman (no.4) for upscale pub fare.

COLLINS
BIRD
GUIDE

4

THE SPORTSMAN

Luxury cabins in the grounds of feted restaurant

If you've never dined at The Sportsman, Seasalter's Michelin-starred gastropub, then you have, by all accounts, missed out. And if the restaurant's five-course tasting menu was already on your bucket list, this quintet of colourful cabins will be right up your street – since it's quite literally on theirs (or, more accurately, in their garden). Each of these roomy lodges has been assigned a different artist and colour palette, and each is appointed with generous living spaces and whimsical beach-hut-style interiors. A veritable treat for foodies, not only do the cabins permit guests to savour an indulgent feast before rolling into bed a few metres away, they also include scrumptious breakfasts when you wake, conveyed to your cabin courtesy of The Sportsman kitchen. The site is also located within easy reach of Whitstable – another culinary utopia for that bucket list.

Faversham Road, Seasalter, Whitstable CT5 4BP

01227 273370

shepherdneame.co.uk

CAMPARI

The cabins are conveniently located in the grounds of the Michelin-starred gastropub, The Sportsman.

DESIGN The Sportsman doesn't advertise or feature pictures of the cabins on its website, so discovering their serene interiors feels like uncovering a well-kept secret. You can get an idea of what lies within from the exteriors, whose bold hues inform the interior schemes – albeit not quite so flamboyantly. Featured designers include Whitstable artist Kimmy McHarries, whose handmade mosaics are displayed on the walls of the marine-themed blue cabin (you can also choose from black, green, red or yellow).

FACILITIES Cabins, each comprising a lounge and dining room, fully equipped kitchen, bathroom with double shower and bedroom with king-sized bed, provide generous space for two people. Free Wi-Fi, a flat-screen TV and a selection of books and boardgames lie in wait for any potential bursts of boredom – though you'll likely be too preoccupied with eating your way through the many delicious dishes to want for anything else. Speaking of which, breakfasts consisting of granola, butter, wholemeal bread, marmalade, local eggs and yoghurt are provided each morning – or for an additional fee you can request all the ingredients needed for a decadent fry-up.

LOCATION The cabins are positioned in The Sportsman's glorious back garden, with views over expanses of wildflowers (not to mention easy access to chef Stephen Harris's exceptional food). A veritable utopia for epicureans, brass lamps and a characterful bridge create the sense that you've truly entered gourmet Narnia.

NEARBY The Sportsman overlooks the Saxon Shore Way coastal footpath, which leads to Whitstable in one direction and Faversham in the other. The views are positively awe-inspiring, though be sure to pack sturdy walking boots as both journeys are quite the hike.

5

BEARSTED LODGE

Chalet-chic within easy reach of London

Tired of London (but not of life)? This chalet-esque cabin is perfectly suited to urbanites without cars, offering a bucolic escape within a short stroll of a London train line. Positioned on the periphery of the ancient village of Bearsted – with its smattering of independent shops, listed buildings and top-rated restaurants – it is restoratively rural without feeling totally cut off. But if it's seclusion you're seeking then it's great for that too, with a big TV for film nights, a huge window above the bed for wildlife watching and a hot tub you'll want to soak in until you resemble a prune. Woodland surroundings, wood-clad walls and 1970s Scandi decor amp up the Alpine vibes, transporting you even further from the M25 (spiritually at least – in reality it's just 25 miles down the road).

The Pines, Sutton Street, Bearsted ME14 4HP
airbnb.co.uk

DESIGN Hygge feels abound at this cosy cabin, where warm wood panels and eclectic vintage furniture combine to create a delightfully nostalgic 1970s ski-lodge ambiance. A low-height mezzanine sleeping area ups the snug factor, with a large skylight window allowing twilight owl-watching and stargazing from the comfort of the futon mattress bed. In the colder months underfloor heating offers a toasty-toed treat, while in the summer the bifold doors can be flung open to summon nature in.

FACILITIES A true home from home where every eventuality has been pre-empted, the cabin includes a kitchenette complete with toaster, kettle, Nespresso machine, hob and microwave. An outdoor barbeque permits lazy al fresco feasts in the summer and marshmallow toasting in the winter, with garden furniture including sun loungers available, weather permitting. And if it doesn't permit, you can snuggle down in front of that (Roku-enabled) big TV instead.

LOCATION Located in the corner of hosts Barbara and Mike Chandler's 1.5-acre garden, 60 metres from their own home, the cabin might not feel quite as secluded as others but that doesn't make it any less relaxing. On the contrary, the garden's sprawling canopy of trees and luxurious deck-top hot tub (which, while not totally hidden from view, comes with exclusive access) make a stay at Bearsted one of the most tranquil getaways you can experience this close to London.

NEARBY As well as all the amenities of Bearsted village, there are numerous idyllic woodland walks beginning at the front door. If you have a car, the historic Leeds Castle is just five minutes away, while a drive to the Kent coast will take 40-60 minutes, depending on what kind of beach vibe you're looking for. Top Bearsted picks include The Oak on the Green gastropub, The White Horse pub, the Michelin-listed Fish on the Green seafood restaurant and the top-rated Crouch butchers and delicatessen.

6

KOYA, UNPLUGGED

72-hour digital detox for urbanites

Ever felt like the only way to escape Instagram's vice-like grip on your attention would be to lock your phone away in a box? This ingenious cabin concept allows you to do just that for three long, dreamy days. Conceived by two burnt-out tech professionals following one of their returns from a Himalayan retreat, Unplugged hideaways offer a wonderfully simple antidote to a hectic urban life, with 15 remote locations (to date) within two hours' drive or train of London, and another three near Manchester. Once inside, stow your phone away in a specially designed lockbox and replace your screen with paper maps and real-life conversations – or, failing that, just staring blankly out of the (massive) window. Koya is the original of the collection, offering a completely off-grid experience surrounded by ancient farmland, but still within an hour's drive of north London. And don't worry – you do get your phone back when the three days are up.

Arkesden, Saffron Walden CB11
unplugged.rest

Koya can be found close to Audley End, one of the most beautiful and culturally important estates in the UK.

DESIGN As with all cabins in the Unplugged collection, Koya's interior is minimalist but comfortable, entirely clad with stylish birch ply and with panoramic windows that fully immerse you in the spectacular surroundings. The cabin's compact footprint contrasts with the expanse of unspoilt countryside enveloping it, emphasising the sense of solitude, while its understated black satin exterior (not to mention its eco-friendly compostable toilet, solar-panel power system and exclusive use of low-carbon materials) is sympathetic to its ancient environs.

FACILITIES All cabins come elegantly equipped with everything you need – but nothing you don't – for a three-night flight from reality. From luxury essentials (including a king-size bed with Piglet in Bed linen, a hot rainforest shower, eco-friendly toiletries, coffee beans and grinder) through to off-grid treats (including a cassette player and mix tapes, an analogue map, board games, an instant camera, an old-school Nokia loaded with emergency numbers and the all-important lockbox), everything has been painstakingly considered.

LOCATION Despite their relative proximity to cities, the cabins' locations have all been selected for their remoteness and sense of total immersion in nature, whether it's on the edge of a country farm surrounded by rolling hills or shrouded in peaceful woodland. Koya is situated on a chicken farm close to Audley End, and access requires abandoning your car at the end of a lane and walking the final stretch – which only adds to that feeling of delicious isolation.

NEARBY Try The Cricketers in Clavering for award-winning seasonal food, or venture further afield to the stunning medieval town of Saffron Walden, which is home to the majestic Audley End mansion and its Capability Brown-designed gardens, the elegant Bridge End Garden (with its mystifying hedge maze) and the half-timbered Tudor gastropub The Eight Bells.

7

RADAR

Otherworldly escape with unique 'desert' backdrop

Erected on the site of two derelict sheds built in the 1960s to test radar equipment, this one-of-a-kind retreat acts as a lavish theatre to the eerie magnificence of Dungeness. Like the landscape it inhabits, Radar is strange but beautiful, comprising a brown corrugated-metal shell and a minimalist interior in various shades of grey. Its lavish sunken bath, on-site sauna and east- and west-facing terraces (one for sunrises and one for sunsets) make it ideal for romantic retreats, but it will appeal just as much to architecture-loving friends or lone travellers seeking solitude. There's plenty to see on Dungeness, from the late artist and gay-rights activist Derek Jarman's garden to the miniature Romney, Hythe and Dymchurch Railway, the 600+ species of plants that thrive in spite of the hostile climate and endless fascinating remnants of a dead technology. If you want to experience it all in style, this is the one to book.

Dungeness, Romney Marsh TN29 9NB
bloomstays.com

DESIGN Radar's interiors blend seamlessly with the scenery, comprising wood panelling and textiles the same hue as the shingle beach. Minimalistic yet luxurious, with every comfort considered, the cabin enjoys underfloor heating throughout and warm walls in the shower, as well as a separate, spa-like bathroom and beautiful panelled sauna. Outside, the interlocking pitched roofs reference the pair of sheds that once stood on the site, while decks to the front and rear allow guests to make the most of Dungeness's epic dawns and dusks.

FACILITIES Despite its unfussy decor, Radar comes fully furnished with everything you'll need for a calm and comfortable stay. The open-plan living space includes a surprisingly well-equipped kitchen, a serene sitting area complete with cosy sofa, armchair and wood burner and even a king-sized bed up on the mezzanine – though with a privacy curtain to create a more partitioned feel if needed.

LOCATION The Dungeness Nature Reserve is an endlessly fascinating place to visit, possessing an intense energy that's at once beguiling and unnerving. Often said to be the only desert in the UK (though it doesn't technically qualify due to the high levels of rainfall), the location has attracted countless artists and architects over the years – and it's not hard to see why. Radar itself is positioned on a public shingle beach, affording it enviable views across the landscape. The neighbouring lighthouse is still operational and sounds fog warning signals when necessary, but that just adds to the eccentric charm of the place.

NEARBY Dungeness Snack Shack serves delectable lobster rolls and crab flatbreads, while the fish hut next door sells fresh fish to cook at home. The Dungeness shoreline isn't suitable for swimming, but there are plenty of nearby beaches that are, if you fancy a change of scenery – though the miniature railway and Derek Jarman's house with its free-to-roam garden are both within walking distance if you don't.

From the cabin, it's possible to visit The Old Lighthouse and Derek Jarman's Prospect Cottage. For lunch, stop off for a scallop roll from Dungeness Snack Shack.

8

KUDHVA

Unique treetop 'camping' pods

Perched peculiarly above the trees like the abandoned spaceships of some technologically advanced alien race, this quartet of two-person cabins is unique to say the least. Part of Kudhva's self-labelled 'landscape hotel', the treehouse-like structures offer a dramatically different way to camp in the wild. Providing the feeling of sleeping in a tent while being infinitely more interesting (and lofty), their huge windows look out across a lush woodland canopy or the beautiful Cornish coast. As you'd expect of a regular campsite, the shower and cooking facilities are communal and located a short walk away, but that's all part of the Kudhva experience, which feels like something everyone should try at least once in their lifetime. Great if you're looking for somewhere a little (or a lot) different.

Sanding Road, Trebarwith Strand,
Tintagel, Cornwall PL34 0HH
07917 735244
kudhva.com

The Kudhva site's shared kitchen also includes a long communal dinner table, ideal for meeting others at the retreat.

DESIGN Stark and yet strangely beautiful, these prototype structures perch on stilts high above the ground, reachable via a metal staircase. Collectively called 'Kudhva', the cabins are individually designated K1, K2, K3 and K4 – labels that speak to their sci-fi design. A comfortable sofa, mezzanine bed and huge triangular window are all you get (and all you need) here, in a landscape that does all the talking.

FACILITIES Each cabin comes complete with fresh linen and towels, as well as everything you need to whip up a hearty cooked breakfast each morning. Prepare yours over your own private firepit or head along the winding path to the rustic communal kitchen, located at the Kudhva reception building. Here you'll also find hot showers, flushing toilets and plug sockets, should you need them.

LOCATION Each pod enjoys the same spectacular woodland landscape as The Danish Cabin, albeit with slightly different locations and outlooks. Opt for K1 or K4 for iconic sea views, or K2 or K3 for verdant forest vistas. The Kudhva site has plenty to explore, including a wild swimming lake, a waterfall, a climbing wall and a hot tub.

NEARBY Wander the ethereal Atlantic coastline, known for its rugged beauty and incredible sunsets, explore the ancient ruins of Tintagel Castle or head to Outlaw's Fish Kitchen in nearby Port Isaac for globally inspired, locally sourced fish dishes in a 15th-century former fisherman's cottage.

The pods are only a short hike away from the delightfully rugged Cornish coast, but if you're not in the mood for a bracing sea dip, there are wood-fired hot tubs on site.

9

THE DANISH CABIN

Off-grid hideaway in otherworldly landscape

So called because it was originally built for multinational brewers Carlsberg, The Danish Cabin offers an out-of-this-world glamping experience that needs to be lived to be believed. Situated in a 43-acre disused slate quarry on the north coast of Cornwall, the off-grid cabin has been experimentally designed to immerse guests in the wild surroundings, positioned on stilts among the trees and with walls that fold up to expose you to the elements. A 1:3 wooden replica of the site's Grade II-listed engine house, the cabin is ideal for groups of friends with its six beds, in-house bar (a throwback to its Carlsberg days) and wealth of activities on and offsite, from dips in the wood-fired hot tub to sound baths held in a tipi, as well as surf trips to nearby Trebarwith Strand – one of the most impressive beaches in North Cornwall.

Sanding Road, Trebarwith Strand,
Tintagel, Cornwall PL34 0HH
07917 735244
kudhva.com

Can Crusher

An ideal escape for nature-lovers, the cabin's walls fold up, ushering the forest in. It's also possible to explore the vast disused slate quarry that surrounds the cabin by raft.

DESIGN The Danish Cabin is one of the spaces offered by self-styled landscape hotel Kudhva. *Kudhva* means hideout in Cornish, and you couldn't feel more hidden from humanity than when camped out among the trees in this effortlessly cool cabin. The veil between exterior and interior is thin here, with stripped-back interiors and fold-up walls making it hard to tell where one ends and the other begins – but that's all part of the fun of this wonderfully wild resort.

FACILITIES Amenities here are deliberately scant, allowing you to decelerate and connect with your surroundings. The two sofas turn into beds at night, and there's also a bunk room with four further beds. There's no heating or Wi-Fi on the site, which is closed November to March, and the solar-powered communal showers and cooking space are an atmospheric ten-minute walk through the forest, with breakfast hampers available to order.

LOCATION Guests must complete a short hike to reach the Kudhva site, making it feel all the more special and secluded when you arrive. The cabin itself sits within lush woodland, a short distance from a 40-metre waterfall and quarry where you can wild swim or float around the water on a rustic wooden raft.

NEARBY Kudhva regularly hosts guest chefs, pop ups and long-table feasts. Supposing nothing's scheduled when you arrive, amble 30 minutes to Trebarwith gastropubs The Port William or The Mill House Inn, or try Outlaw's Fish Kitchen in Port Isaac, just 20 minutes away by car. You're unlikely to want to drag yourself far from your private deck, which has a tranquil stream running beneath it, but in case you do there are virtually endless coastal walks and surfing opportunities in the vicinity.

Stroll ten minutes through the forest to the hub of the Kudhva site, the communal kitchen.

PLACES TO EAT

10

HULDER CABIN

Scandinavian-style sanctuary for romantic retreats

Whether taking its name from Old Devonian (where *hulder* means to hide or conceal) or from the hulder of Norse mythology (one of nature's wardens, a seductive forest being who spends her days hidden among the trees), this cabin lives up to the moniker. Tucked away in the Devon countryside and masterfully constructed from cedar, larch and Douglas fir, the generously proportioned Hulder offers a restful base for two, with plenty of cosy corners housed under the beamed ceiling, including a beautiful platform bed complete with a shelf full of books and a copper bath beneath the covered deck. The ultimate hibernation spot, whatever the season, the Hulder Cabin is so well-equipped you'll barely need to set foot off the deck unless you want to – though if you do, all the quiet delights of North Devon are just beyond the trees.

Marsh Farm, Cheriton Fitzpaine,
Crediton EX17 4BD
kiphideaways.com

BEN STOKES
WILDING
Chess
Under the Stars

DESIGN Above and beyond your average holiday hut, the Hulder Cabin benefits from a stunning bespoke design that's straight out of Scandinavia, employing locally sourced materials with careful consideration of the interior style. But it's not just a pretty face; the building has also been intelligently engineered with the latest eco technology to ensure it's as energy efficient as possible, while floor-to-ceiling windows that open fully onto the terrace to make the most of the Devon skies.

FACILITIES From a complimentary local produce hamper to an outdoor cooking area and deck-top firepit poised for toasty late-night chats, the Hulder Cabin's hosts have thought of everything (except for Wi-Fi and a TV, which have been deliberately omitted and we guarantee you won't miss).

LOCATION Buried in a quiet field on a blissfully remote farm in rural Devon, the Hulder Cabin is about as serene as it gets – save for the sounds of the deer, kingfishers, otters, barn owls and other creatures that also call this part of the world home.

NEARBY The delightful Ring of Bells pub in Cheriton Fitzpaine is a 20-minute walk from the cabin, while the equally excellent Cadeleigh Arms near Tiverton is just a ten-minute drive away. Spitchwick in Dartmoor is a popular spot for wild swimming, and there's a magnificent circular walk from Fingle Bridge, with several swimming opportunities en route. You're also relatively close to Exeter, Fursdon House and Gardens and the sandy beaches of North Devon.

Bathe with a view over the blissfully remote Devon farm where the cabin is situated.

Spend an evening toasting marshmallows over the deck-top firepit.

11

LAKESIDE CABIN

Lakeside haven well-placed for St Ives

Known for its world-class galleries and great surfing beaches, picturesque St Ives frequently exceeds capacity in the summer months – and with good reason. But if the hordes have previously put you off booking a Cornish getaway, this award-winning retreat might just change your mind. Set in serene farmland overlooking a tranquil lake, but with all the hustle and bustle just 20 minutes by car, the Boat House offers the best of both worlds, with plenty to stimulate your brain and soothe your soul on the doorstep. Along with a rowing boat poised for self-guided tours of the lake, the spacious cabin comprises a sprawling deck that overhangs the water, with an outdoor bathtub, comfy furniture and welcoming firepit – the perfect blend of culture and calm.

Pengelly Mill, Drym, Leedstown, Hayle TR27 6BW
01736 850225
kiphideaways.com

Gwithian beach, just a 20-minute drive from the cabin, is ideal for surfing, or if you'd rather stay put, the cabin has its own private boating lake.

DESIGN The cabin's generous living space, lofty ceilings and neutral decor provide an idyllic backdrop for a relaxing stay, with large windows allowing endless light to flood in and bifold doors extending the inside space out onto the cantilevered deck. Sitting just off the living area, the bedroom's sky lights and vaulted ceiling create a sense of airy luxury, added to by the plush double bed and ensuite shower room. Bright pops of colour and soft textiles add a layer of warmth, making the interior feel cosy even in the cooler months.

FACILITIES The Boat House goes above and beyond, comprising a well-equipped kitchen prepped with everything you need to make a delicious breakfast and an ensuite complete with complimentary toiletries. Underfloor heating, a contemporary log burner and film projector kit (bring your own laptop) make the cabin just as perfect for wintry retreats, and you can elevate your experience by ordering a Cornish food box, or even booking a holistic treatment or yoga session to enjoy from the privacy of the deck.

LOCATION Positioned six miles southeast of the port town of Hayle and 11 miles from St Ives, this stunning lakeside retreat feels simultaneously blissfully remote and excellently connected, allowing you to experience all the buzz of the Cornish coast without the sensory overwhelm. As well as access to your own private boating lake, stays include use of the adjacent secret garden (home to tropical plants and hidden Buddha statues), as well stunning woodland walks on the doorstep.

NEARBY Ten minutes away by car, Hayle is home to top-rated chocolate-box pub the Cornish Arms, along with three glorious miles of golden sandy beaches. A further ten minutes down the road, arty St Ives hosts illustrious galleries including the Tate and the Barbara Hepworth Museum and Gardens, as well as the famous Leach pottery and SILCo Sea Room for phenomenal seafood and cocktails. Or, if it's surfing that entices you, grab your board and head for the shores of Gwithian or Godrevy on the north coast, or Praa Sands to the south.

12

NORTH DEVON HIDEAWAY

Off-grid retreat in upcycled farm building

Once a dilapidated cattle shed, this beguiling barn has been sensitively converted into a soulful off-grid haven. Located in its own private valley surrounded by acres of shady woodland, vibrant wildflower meadows and babbling streams, the cabin offers a wonderfully cleansing stay, free from electricity or Wi-Fi, providing the ideal setting for reconnecting with loved ones away from the stresses of modern life. Small but perfectly formed, with a strong character that belies its footprint, the hideaway will focus your attention on life's littlest pleasures, from enjoying a game of Scrabble to the traditional Devon cream tea with scones that greets you on arrival. With space to sleep two kids, this hideaway is perfect for families as well as couples – or anyone you're happy sharing a small space with.

Butterhills, Braunton EX33 2NJ
kiphideaways.com

The well-equipped kitchen makes this a great place to cook some comfort food or even try out new recipes.

DESIGN The cabin's owners could easily have built it from scratch, but in upcycling the existing farm building they've created a substantially more interesting structure. Abounding with texture, the open-plan cabin combines rugged stone walls with smooth wood panelling and wool blankets, while solar lighting, sustainable grub and taps served by a well add to the rustic charm.

FACILITIES There's a lot packed into this tiny space, but the vibe is considerably more 'cosy' than 'poky'. The kitchen has been kitted out for serious cooks and bakers, making this a great place to test out those recipes you've been meaning to try. As well as a futon, there's a mezzanine bed up in the eaves, while outside there's a large dining table, a hammock for reading and a firepit surrounded by benches. You can also make use of an open outdoor hut when you long to be immersed in nature but the weather is not on your side, as well as a selection of board games and guidebooks.

LOCATION The cabin is enviably positioned in a peaceful woodland glade, surrounded by mature oak trees and near a rippling stream. Pack a pair of binoculars to catch a glimpse of the resident foxes, badgers and otters from that hammock. Bliss.

NEARBY The local village pub and shop are both within walking distance, with the latter even offering a handy home-delivery service. The golden sands of North Devon's beaches are just five miles away, with paddleboards available to hire, and you can also rent bikes and cycle the Tarka Trail. Head to the car-free village of Clovelly and pick up some fresh fish from Dan the Fish Man, or to Barricane Beach to visit the little hut that becomes a Sri Lankan restaurant after 5pm.

13

BOWCOMBE BOATHOUSE

Characterful waterside sanctuary

The end result of owner Miranda Gardiner's decades spent collecting artefacts as a painter and curator, Bowcombe feels more like an artist's clifftop hideaway than a holiday rental. The subject of many a high-end interiors magazine, the cabin is tastefully furnished with salvage-yard finds. Occupying a former boat store on the edge of a beautiful ria, rental includes the use of two kayaks, enabling magical paddles to neighbouring Kingsbridge. Such a private location makes this feel like a getaway in the deepest sense, with a well-stocked drinks cabinet and inviting window nook offering a home-from-home vibe, and heavy wooden gates forming a physical and psychological barrier between the cabin and the rest of the world (though with the many charms of Kingsbridge waiting just beyond them, should you want them).

Embankment Road, Kingsbridge TQ7 4DR
canopyandstars.co.uk

The Bowcombe Boathouse sits on the Kingsbridge estuary, which is visible from every window of the property.

DESIGN Bowcombe's interiors are so characterful that staying in them almost makes you feel like Goldilocks trespassing on someone else's momentarily deserted property. Collected over Miranda's long career as an artist, the property's one-of-a-kind antique furnishings, unusual knick knacks and numerous nods to its estuary location are set against wood-panelled walls to create the ultimate waterside hideaway.

FACILITIES The groaning drinks cabinet, lovingly stocked with a selection of local gins and rums, is a welcome highlight of this charming cabin. Pour yourself a tipple and take a scenic seat on the veranda (firepit optional) or light the log burner and curl up in the window with a good book. Guests also enjoy the use of a full kitchen, lounge and dining space, as well as an upstairs bedroom and bathroom with magnificent sea views from the shower.

LOCATION The location of Bowcombe is hard to beat, with the Kingsbridge estuary visible from every part of the property. A set of metal steps offer direct access to the water beneath, allowing for easy-going paddles into Kingsbridge or even wild swimming at high tide.

NEARBY Despite the sense of seclusion, you're only a five-minute walk from the picturesque Crabshell Inn with its moreish seafood and wood-fired pizzas, and a few glorious minutes' paddle (or a ten-minute walk) from pretty Kingsbridge, where you can moor up and head to a plethora of cafes and restaurants. Alternatively, grab your walking boots and discover one of Devon's many coastal walks, or even the wilds of Dartmoor.

14

BUCK'S COPPICE

Off-grid cabin with secluded swimming

Ever dreamt of wild swimming in your own private lake? What about a private lake connected to your own private eco-cabin, which, despite being off-grid, offers the utmost comfort with its spacious living areas and Scandi-chic furnishings? In fact, with its picturesque location, all clear waters and ancient woodland, Buck's Coppice feels more like a summerhouse on the Stockholm Archipelago than a cabin in the depths of the Dorset countryside, making it ideal for romantic retreats – and particularly special occasions. That said, the sofa bed sleeps two children, and you can even tootle around the water in a paddle boat if cold-water bathing isn't your thing. However you choose to do it and whoever you choose to do it with, you're guaranteed a memorable stay here, with plenty to see off-site if you can drag yourself away.

Buck's Coppice, Beaminster DT8 3PG
07971 784093
canopyandstars.co.uk

The lake on Buck's Coppice's doorstep is suitable for wild swimming and paddleboating.

DESIGN With its high-end Scandi decor, fully equipped kitchen and all the mod cons you could desire, Buck's Coppice dispels the myth that off-grid means basic. On the contrary, the cabin is packed with thoughtful details, from a shelf full of books and stunning original artworks to a pair of binoculars ready for impromptu birdwatching. Beautiful both outside and in, the wood-clad building enjoys triple-aspect views over the tranquil lake – which will likely be the focus of any stay here.

FACILITIES The lack of electricity is barely noticeable in the cabin, which draws its water from the lake with solar power and employs gas for lighting, cooking and water heating. A flushing toilet and hot shower combined with the roaring log burner make stays in the colder months almost as alluring as summer sojourns, and there's even a stack of games ready for chilled evenings in.

LOCATION Buck's Coppice enjoys a wonderfully remote location in an Area of Scientific Interest within the Dorset Area of Outstanding Natural Beauty. In addition to the swimmable lake, the cabin includes a large wraparound viewing deck with comfortable sofa seating, from which it's possible to spot a wide variety of local bird life, as well as deer, wild boar, badgers and otters.

NEARBY For seaside charm head to Lyme Regis or West Bay. Or for gift shops and farmers' markets, drive less than 20 minutes to pretty Beaminster or bustling Bridport. If it's history you want, the Jacobean Mapperton House and Gardens is just a five-minute drive away and boasts stunningly landscaped gardens, a great cafe and even a resident tortoise.

15

CATKINS HUTS

Opulent hideaways with indie hotel vibes

Craving a cabin escape but can't function without home comforts? This quartet of luxe Dorset farm hideaways might be right up your street (or blissfully far from it). Combining the reflective solitude of a cabin with the comfortable extravagance of a boutique hotel, each hut – two regular, two XL (extra-luxe) – is a glorious cacophony of pattern and bold colours that combine to create a self-styled 'English maximalist' vibe. From brass drinks trolleys to welcome hampers and open-air baths to handmade headboards, everything about Catkins feels fabulously extra. And with heaps to do on the doorstep, from wild swimming and epic country walks to the delights of the Jurassic Coast and Langham wine estate just a short drive away, it's fair to say the fun factor is pretty maximalist too.

Near Milton Abbas, Dorset DT11
kiphideaways.com

DESIGN The huts' small footprints haven't stopped owners Cat and Ant Bugler from making a big statement when it comes to their interiors. Whether you opt for a standard or XL cabin, bold colour and print set the tone, with colourful cabinets and vibrant upholstery harmonising to create a fun yet cohesive, high-end look. Keep an eye out for fashion alumni Cat's hand-upholstered headboards, which have proved so popular with guests you can even order one for your own home.

FACILITIES Huts are equipped with full kitchens, and welcome hampers stuffed with locally sourced essentials greet guests on arrival. You'll even find a brass drinks trolley stocked with everything you need to mix up a punchy cocktail. Outside each cabin you'll discover your own elegant hot tub (the XL tubs are surrounded by tiled walls), as well as a roaring firepit where you can toast marshmallows or cook a barbecue dinner. A rainforest shower, thick bath robes, upmarket bath products, underfloor heating and a flushing loo up the luxe factor, while meat and vegetable boxes are available to order from local suppliers. Or, if you're feeling fancy, you can commission your own personal chef to whip up a lobster thermidor on site.

LOCATION Set around a picturesque lake on the Buglers' family farm in West Dorset's Marshwood Vale, the Catkins huts are the perfect base for some wild swimming. Don't worry if you don't fancy taking the plunge, though – there are also countless spectacular walks to be enjoyed in the surrounding area. Or just sit back and take in the views – either on a lounger by the lake or in a frothy hot tub under the stars. You can even hire a local yoga instructor to give you a lesson from the comfort of your cabin.

NEARBY Catkins is just a half-hour drive from the golden sands of Studland Bay on Dorset's magnificent Jurassic Coast. Book ahead for lunch at Studland's whimsical The Pig on the Beach hotel, or show up unannounced for one of their famous flatbread pizzas. Nearby Bridport and Beaminster are both great for antique shops and boutiques, and the legendary Langham wine estate – famed for its award-winning sparkling wine – runs regular tours and tastings.

THE ROASTING TIN
SIMPLY
OTTOLENGHI SIMPLE

Cabins come complete with welcome hampers full of locally sourced treats.

16

AUTHOR'S ESCAPE

Former writer's home by the sea

Once the home of *Tarka the Otter* author Henry Williamson, this soulful property is endlessly inspiring, nestled within the Devon landscape that informed the novel and offering exclusive access to the writing shed Williamson built in the garden. Meticulously renovated down to its original shell, the house combines all the conveniences and energy efficiency of a modern property with the quirky charisma of a much older one – the latter enhanced by the current owner's inclusion of various interesting artworks and objects, and the fact that Williamson wrote three of his books in the cosy downstairs bedroom. Writing stimulus aside, the garden shed is a perfectly pickled piece of history, preserved as Williamson left it before he died. The site is also impeccably placed for Devon's best surfing beaches, supposing you're more into boards than books.

Georgeham, Croyde, Braunton EX33 1HX
kiphideaways.com

Once the home of Henry Williamson, the cabin's current owner has filled the space with quirky atefacts.

The writing shed in the garden has been preserved as a tribute to former resident Henry Williamson, whose novels were inspired by the natural world.

DESIGN More house than cabin, this spacious property is ideal for family escapes, with two roomy bedrooms and a large open-plan living area with a vaulted ceiling, kitchen island and huge dining table. The modern interiors are sympathetic to the building's heritage, while statement beds and flashes of colour add to the already rich sense of character, along with unusual trinkets scattered throughout (the monkey-shaped candlesticks a particular favourite). The writing shed, by contrast, is very much a time warp, and provides a great place to gather inspiration, even if you're not permitted to sleep there.

FACILITIES Supposing you're not too busy penning your next novel, pull down the large projector screen and spend an evening curled up in front of a film. The cabin boasts its own water supply from a bore-hole, along with high-level insulation (meaning heating is rarely required) – though there is a log burner for particularly chilly evenings.

LOCATION Perched on the edge of the North Devon Area of Outstanding Natural Beauty, the cabin enjoys breathtaking views over Woolacombe Beach's turquoise waters. It also falls within a Dark Sky Discovery Site, making it a magical spot for stargazing on warm evenings.

NEARBY The astonishingly vast Croyde Bay and Saunton Sands are both a short drive (or longer hike) away and both highly rated for surfing. Or, if you prefer terra firma, there are endless ambles to be had on nearby Exmoor. The award-winning Rock Inn is also within walking distance, offering freshly caught fish in an intimate setting, and there are plenty of fabulous farm shops nearby if you prefer to do the cooking yourself.

17

FIREFLY

Rustic carpenter's cabin close to Cornish coast

Its owners' ambition to turn an old stable building into a replica of a turn-of-the-century woodcutter's workshop has been so successfully realised in Firefly, you might feel like you've accomplished time travel. Nestled in the Cornish hamlet of Trebudannon, between popular Newquay and pretty Mawgan Porth, this cleverly crafted cabin inspires a relaxed return to the simple life – though without compromising on luxury. In the unlikely event you tire of wildlife watching by the pond, feasting by the firepit and enjoying lengthy dips in the dreamy hot tub, there are countless sandy beaches, incredible Cornish seafood and some of the UK's best surfing spots mere minutes away. Or why not elevate your escape with a soothing massage or chef-cooked meal from the comfort of the cabin?

Stanley Lain House, Trebudannon,
Newquay TR8 4LP
01637 881183
uniquehomestays.com

Designed to mimic a century-old woodcutter's workshop, the cabin is full of handcrafted charm.

DESIGN Firefly has been so skilfully designed it doesn't take much to imagine its woodcutter inhabitants living here – even if they're entirely fictional. Carpentry tools dangle from the kitchen island, while animal skulls are displayed on the wall like trophies, augmenting the narrative along with vintage books and handmade pottery. Honest materials such as rope, an abundance of reclaimed age-worn wood and the recycled corrugated iron sheets used for the roof and shower create a real sense of lived-in warmth, with draped furs and thick curtains and bedding upping the cosy factor.

FACILITIES The open-plan living space is the beating heart of Firefly and comes complete with a top-of-the-range Aga and open fire. The fully equipped kitchen includes a vintage Belfast sink and dishwasher, while the living-room area boasts a velvet sofa, a 'hidden' smart TV with Freeview and Netflix, a Sonos sound system and an iPad, plus Wi-Fi. Outside you'll find a spacious veranda with a firepit, luxurious hot tub and wildlife pond, and you can even book a beauty treatment or private chef.

LOCATION Immersed in countryside less than a 20-minute drive from Newquay, Firefly offers the perfect base for exploring the Cornish coast and moors. Its fully enclosed garden makes it ideal for dog owners and vast barn doors create a free-flowing indoor-outdoor living space.

NEARBY As well as offering dog-friendly countryside walks on the doorstep and breath-taking coastal hikes just 15 minutes away, Firefly is perfectly positioned for the spectacular Bedruthan Steps Beach, the 18-mile Camel Trail cycling route, scuba diving with Dive Newquay and Rick Stein's illustrious seafood restaurants.

18

THE TREE HOUSE

Grown-up retreat with playful allure

Unfulfilled childhood dreams of lofty treehouse dens are brought to life at this whimsical Cotswold hideaway, whose lavish interiors and out-of-this-world surroundings may have you wondering if you are in fact still dreaming. Wildly romantic – though located opposite a two-bed coach house holiday home, making it good for bringing extended families, too – the Tree House is impeccably placed for exploring the Cotswolds' pretty, chocolate-box villages, with bountiful walks, antiques shops and stately homes at your feet. Situated in the glorious grounds of a 17th-century country house, this treetop hideout possesses a grandeur that belies its tiny footprint with its luxurious fixtures, opulent velvet sofa, sizable deck and extravagant freestanding bath. If you're looking for a getaway that's extra special, it might be time to get your head in the clouds.

Bagpath, Tetbury, Gloucestershire GL5
sandandstoneescapes.com

DESIGN The cabin has been exquisitely handcrafted from solid oak and cedar by artisan carpenters to create a rustic treehouse feel, with established trees growing through the wraparound deck and a tree-trunk staircase for added authenticity. Spread across two levels, it comprises an open-plan lounge with luxury wood burner for chillier days and vast trifold doors that can be flung back on warmer ones, extending the living space onto the deck. Up in the eaves, the triangular bedroom window offers a bird's-eye view of the treetops from the sumptuous comfort of the king-sized bed, while the luxuriously tiled bathroom invites invigorating showers and long soaks after busy days spent exploring.

FACILITIES Begin your stay as you mean to go on with a complimentary hamper bursting with local treats and a bottle of bubbly that's best enjoyed in the freestanding bath. The bathroom is a highlight of the cabin, comprising a tiled shower, twin sinks, luxury Bamford products and bifold doors that open onto the deck. Outside you can experience an al fresco shower among the trees, or simply recline on the sprawling outdoor sofa to the relaxing sound of birdsong. On cooler evenings, cosy up on the velvet sofa for a night in front of the 55-inch TV, which transforms into an artwork when not in use.

LOCATION Nestled in the heart of the Cotswolds countryside, five miles southwest of Tetbury, the Tree House offers panoramic views of an Area of Outstanding Natural Beauty, spanning tranquil lakes, rolling hills and endless greenery. Its breathtaking raised deck is the ultimate place to unwind, comprising a barbecue, swing chair and birdfeeder primed for visits from feathered friends.

NEARBY The 16th-century Hunter's Hall Inn is a 20-minute walk along a country lane, while Tetbury's antique boutiques and 18th-century Royal Oak pub are all a five-minute drive away. There's a wonderful circular walk that begins on the doorstep and winds through the Lasborough and Ozelworth valleys, while the Woodchester Valley Vineyard, Highgrove Gardens and Westonbirt Arboretum are all less than 20 minutes by car.

The two-bed coach house holiday home opposite the cabin is also available to book.

The Tree House is situated in the Cotswolds Area of Outstanding Natural Beauty.

19

ARCHITECT'S HUT

Tiny cabin with impressive eco credentials

This striking cabin's contemporary facade and trend-lend Scandi interior somehow perfectly complements its ancient, unspoilt surroundings, as befits its eco-friendly design which aims to make sure that the beautiful countryside remains unspoilt. Ideal for weekend sequestration, this retreat comes surprisingly well-equipped for its size, with built-in furniture to maximise space and a focus on minimising the carbon footprint as much as the physical one. A king-size bed, top-of-the-range waterless toilet and restaurant-grade pizza oven (with ingredients provided by a local pizzeria) elevate the experience to the point that you could happily stay on site for your entire trip, though the proximity to novelist Thomas Hardy's house and the nearby vineyard's tours and tastings might be enough to tempt you from hiding.

Milton Meadow, Milton Road DT11 0DP
07905 181385
kiphideaways.com

DESIGN The Hut's interior feels cool and moody, with concrete-grey walls and shrewd pops of colour. Assembled during lockdown, the cabin has been thoughtfully designed to make the most of the 18m² footprint, with a custom-built wardrobe, bookcase and window seat, plus integrated storage and heating. It's also impressively eco-friendly, showcasing the latest water-saving technologies as well as low-carbon insulation, and with a mattress that's made from recycled denim.

FACILITIES A beautifully curated bookshelf and a projector screen that comes with use of the owner's MUBI membership mean you're unlikely to get bored. The kitchen may be smaller than other cabins, but this pint-sized space is still complete with a fridge, mini oven and two-ring hob ready for whipping up quick suppers, while the outdoor pizza oven and bistro set allows for al fresco feasting. You'll also find a firepit and swing chair overlooking the valley, along with a sleek, black-clad wood-fired hot tub for sundown soaking.

LOCATION Set within a beautiful valley on a working farm close to the village of Milton Abbas, the Architect's Hut enjoys expansive views across rolling pastures and dense woodland, along with its own friendly community of resident cows, sheep and geese.

NEARBY The illustrious Langham Wine Estate cabin is a seven-minute drive from the Architect's Hut, and offers both guided and self-led tastings, as well as an upmarket cafe. Hardy's Cottage, the cob-and-thatch house where the author wrote *Under the Greenwood Tree* and *Far from the Madding Crowd*, is a 16-minute drive. Or strap on your walking boots and take a 30-minute hike through the fields to the award-winning Steeptonbill Farm Shop where you can have a coffee and pick up locally sourced vegetables, meat and cheese.

Situated on a working farm, the cabin offers spectacular views across the Dorset countryside.

The firepit is well-placed for an evening overlooking the valley.

20

SALTWATER CABIN

Stylish 1950s conversion close to the surf

Within splashing distance of Croyde, renowned as one of Devon's best surfing beaches, this black-clad cabin provides stylish accommodation for up to six wave chasers, with the use of two wooden bellyboards included. Expertly remodelled from an original 1950s cabin, the property boasts a stunning interior that melds Scandi chic with mid-century charm in a nod to its beach-chalet heritage. Its three bedrooms make Saltwater particularly great for families (with clever touches including track doors to create a more private living space in the evening), as well as one bunk room and plenty of space indoors and out. That said, its distinctly grown-up finish – with magnificent ceramic tiles, original art and high-end furnishings – makes it just as perfect for mates' escapes. Either way, surf's up!

32 Leadengate Close, Croyde, Braunton EX33 1PT
07765 404452
kiphideaways.com

The cabin is just a short stroll from Croyde Bay beach, one of Devon's best surfing spots.

DESIGN Saltwater's slick black exterior is beautifully complemented by its clean white insides, with bold splashes of fern green and sugared-almond pink creating a sense of playfulness befitting of a surf shack. Picture windows make the most of the surrounding scenery, while huge sliding doors extend the interior out onto the wraparound deck.

FACILITIES More beach bungalow than coastal cabin, Saltwater is better kitted out than your average family home, providing a fully equipped kitchen (complete with dishwasher and tumble dryer), living room with a smart TV and sound bar plus plenty of books, magazines and board games. There's also a travel cot and highchair available for infants.

LOCATION Walk barefoot from the cabin to Croyde Bay beach, a magical spot for surfing, boasting soft, sand and spectacular scenery. Lifeguard-patrolled in the tourist months and with many good surf schools nearby, it's particularly suited to first timers, with high tide providing some ideal beginners' waves. In the garden, there's a hot tub and outdoor shower for your post-surf hose-downs, as well as a barbecue and outdoor table with views across the dunes.

NEARBY The old-world charm of Croyde village, whose summer street-food vans offer many delicious options, is just a five-minute walk away. Alternatively, take a short drive to Squires in Braunton for the best fish and chips, then eat them on Saunton Sands while looking out to sea. Amble along the headland to Baggy Point or, if you're feeling brave, try a spot of coasteering.

21

AURORA

Clapboard cabin on Cornish cliff face

If it's classic beach-hut magic you seek, look no further than this clifftop cabin, which oozes coastal charm in spades – though with all of the drama and none of the naffness. Wedged high on the rockface above Freathy Beach at Cornwall's breathtaking Whitsand Bay, Aurora is an invigorating treat for all the senses, its unfussy interior and triple-aspect windows providing a clean stage from which to witness salty squalls and supernatural sunrises. Such a wild location could easily feel disquieting, and yet here, totally immersed in nature, it is almost impossible not to relax – even when the weather is at its most intense. One for intimate escapes, or when you need reminding of the raw power of Mother Nature.

Aurora, Freathy, Torpoint PL10
uniquehomestays.com

The cabin's spectacular location overlooking Whitsand Bay.

DESIGN Aurora radiates cool seaside charm by the bucketload, with tongue-and-groove panelling, metro tiles and not a single seashell ornament in sight. Stripped back without feeling stark, the white-washed cabin acts like a giant picture frame, capturing the constantly altering loveliness of the Cornish skies – and managing to feel cool and cosy even when it's howling a gale outside. And when it's not? Fling the patio doors open wide and summon that salty sea air in.

FACILITIES The decor might be pared back but Aurora doesn't skimp on luxuries, from underfloor heating to a Nespresso coffee machine for morning lattes and a selection of luxury local produce to greet you on arrival. There's also an all-important Wi-Fi connection and Samsung smart TV for when you feel like battening down the hatches.

LOCATION Winding your way up the coastal path to greet Aurora for the first time, you're already aware that this is a very different kind of getaway. But while you could easily spend your entire stay camped in this cliffside theatre, there's so much to explore down below, from acres of golden sand to world-class surfing opportunities, swimming spots and fishing villages.

NEARBY Mosey down to the historic Devonpoint Inn for delectable potted crab on toast and Cornish pasties before heading over to Patchwork Studios for its packed cultural programme of live music, spoken word and cinema. Alternatively, catch the Cremyll Ferry for a jaunt over to Plymouth to mooch around Admiral's Hard or check out Royal William Yard's numerous buzzy bars, pop-up breweries, galleries and cafes.

22

CYNEFIN RETREATS

Luxe couples' cabins with wraparound views

Its two-person residences might be designated 'luxury glamping pods', but you'll feel more like you're lodging in an indulgent chalet at Cynefin – a Welsh word meaning 'habitat'. With curved walls to the rear and floor-to-ceiling glass doors to the front, this quartet of couples' cabins has been cunningly designed to capitalise on the surrounding vistas, which stretch from the Brecon Beacons in the west to the Black Mountains in the south. A deluxe leather hot tub, majestic firepit and floating king-sized bed make this the perfect spot to snuggle up with your significant other, but there are plenty of romantic excursions at your fingertips too, from antique book-buying sprees in Hay-on-Wye to cosy country pubs and dreamy hikes in the surrounding landscape. Or, if it's a group gathering you're after, check out Cynefin's Luxe Lodges, which comfortably sleep up to five.

Cynefin Retreats, c/o 3 Sheepcote Bungalows,
Hereford HR3 5HU
07908 978477
cynefinretreats.com

Cynefin Retreats' Willow Cabin, which sleeps a couple and up to one child.

DESIGN The views at Cynefin are so epic they completely dictate the design of the cabins, whose long, narrow layouts and almost complete glass walls allow you to witness them from virtually any spot. Similarly, the private deck stretches across the entire length of the facade, with fully sliding doors allowing you to enjoy the great outdoors from the comfort of the plush interior.

FACILITIES 'Glamping' feels like a misnomer at Cynefin. With its Wi-Fi, wood burner, underfloor heating, hot tub, firepit and barbecue grill, plus table and chairs for al fresco dining, it is rather more plush than the term suggests. There's even a cloakroom where you can hide away your muddy boots so they don't spoil the calming aesthetic.

LOCATION Cynefin sits a mile east of the Welsh border, with nothing but undulating hills and dreamy skies as far as the eye can see. Set in capacious grounds, the pods feel delightfully isolated and yet lie close to many tourist hotspots on both sides of the Wye.

NEARBY Both foodies and culture vultures will fall head over heels for Hay-on-Wye, whose myriad bookshops, coffee spots and cute pubs are just three miles up the road (don't miss the Thursday farmers' market and rustic fine-dining restaurant Chapters). For sensation seekers, there's wild swimming and canoeing on the Wye, horse-riding in the Brecon Beacons and plentiful mountain-biking routes.

The Willow Cabin's private deck stretches across the whole length of the facade.

The spacious al fresco hot tub.

23

THE BIVVY

Back-to-basics breaks in an A-frame cabin

If you asked a child to draw a picture of a tent in a field, it probably wouldn't look wildly different to this Shropshire sanctuary, which occupies a quiet spot on owners David and Andrew's family farm. That's not a slight on its appearance (although its name alludes to camping and its construction is appropriately rustic, having been carried out by the brothers using materials found on site), but rather testament to its charm. And while it might have more of a glamping vibe than your average tent with its wood frame, king-sized bed and gas-heated shower, this is still very much a back-to-basics experience, designed to cut through the noise of modern life (namely your phone, which won't connect to Wi-Fi here) and leave you at one with the elements, your loved ones and blissfully little else.

Whitcliffe Farm, Ludlow, Shropshire SY8 2HB
canopyandstars.co.uk

When staying at the Bivvy, you can dine outside with a view of the rolling Shropshire Hills.

DESIGN The Bivvy may feel less 'designed' and more 'cobbled together', but the result is enchanting, nonetheless. Almost everything you see in this A-frame lodge has been repurposed from surplus materials found in the farm's outbuildings, from kitchen shelving made from an old ladder to a rake that's been resourcefully reimagined as shower hanging space, plus plenty else with which to play a game of 'I wonder what this used to be.'

FACILITIES Its no-frills approach makes a night at the Bivvy almost akin to camping in the wilderness, albeit in the cosy comfort of a huge bed dressed with luxurious linens (one of the only new items purchased for the cabin) and with a log burner to warm your cockles. A gas ring hob allows the preparation of one-pot meals and a selection of games, books and cards are provided in lieu of Wi-Fi – though you'll still be able to get signal and can charge your phone and laptop via the charging pack provided. Outside you'll find a kitchen sink, cool box and barbecue grill, as well as a private hot shower and eco-friendly compost toilet. You'll also receive a locally sourced stack of goodies on arrival – a welcome reminder that this is not your average camping holiday.

LOCATION The cabin feels almost entirely unconnected from the farm that hosts it, with nothing but sheep and rolling hills as far as the eye can see. Such a lack of distractions both inside and out really lets you decelerate, freeing you up to appreciate the simpler things, from building an outdoor fire to slowly brewing your morning coffee.

NEARBY Despite the seemingly remote location, the historic market town of Ludlow is just a short stroll across the neighbouring field. There you'll find numerous eateries, including the upscale Charlton Arms, whose modern pub classics have earnt it a Bib Gourmand. Adrenaline chasers can follow one of the many biking trails nearby in Bringewood or hire a canoe for wild adventures on the River Wye.

24

FIFINELLA RETREAT

Magical hideaway that will enchant children

With its wildflower meadows, secret sunken den and windows overlooking the same views that inspired J.R.R. Tolkien, it's little surprise that Fifinella feels more than slightly Hobbiton-esque. Close to the border with Wales, this one-of-a-kind cabin enjoys incredible mountain vistas of the Brecon Beacons in one direction and the Malvern Hills the other. Designed and built as a lockdown project by owner Zac, Fifinella benefits from a unique open-plan layout that makes the most of every inch of space, with clever partitions that create distinct living areas and birch ply panelling throughout. Particularly great for families, this Scandi-style retreat incorporates everything you could need for a magical escape with kids, from a top-of-the-line barbecue and pizza oven to a built-in projector for cosy film nights in the den. Just keep an eye out for hobbits.

Orcop Treetops, The Woodlands,
Orcop, Hereford HR2 8SE
canopyandstars.co.uk

The cabin enjoys wonderful views of sunset over the England-Wales border.

DESIGN Uniformly clad in birch ply, Fifinella has a laid-back Scandinavian character that's echoed in the Eames dining set, sheepskin throws and pared-back fittings. The glass frontage floods the space with light, creating a strong sense of space and calm, and everything feels beautifully proportioned, with each area slotting together seamlessly like a Soma cube so that there's no wasted space.

FACILITIES Despite a relatively small footprint, the cabin manages to accommodate a double bedroom, walk-in shower, fully equipped kitchen, separate lounge and dining areas and a sunken tatami room, without ever feeling cramped. Outside on the deck you'll find a barbecue-pizza oven, and beyond that a wood-fired hot tub, firepit and enticing hammock. All guests receive a welcome hamper chockfull of local goodies, while vegetables are usually available from the garden and freshly baked bread, eggs and honey can be ordered on-site.

LOCATION Set in peaceful woodland among rolling hills, Fifinella has the very best of the Welsh and Herefordshire countryside at its disposal. Guests can arrange grooming sessions with the adjacent paddock's friendly resident horses or even sign up to feed the 'tiddling' lambs in springtime.

NEARBY Fifinella is ideally placed for exploring the delights of Hay-on-Wye, with ample opportunities for kayaking, canoeing and wild swimming in the river – or just a browse around the town's bookshops if water sports aren't your thing. Drive up nearby Garway Hill to see the sun set over seven counties or stroll to the neighbouring Fountain Inn for tasty Thai cuisine.

25

THE HUDNALLS HIDEOUT

Lavish treehouse set in private woodland

A hideout in the deepest sense, this spectacular treehouse feels deliciously secluded, buried in the treetops of its own private two-acre forest, and with exclusive access to a magical wildflower meadow. Perfect for honeymoons, the property offers generous accommodation for couples, with a tub for two on the deck and a dreamy bedroom in the eaves. Its luxury interior is a far cry from your average cabin in the woods, with cosy underfloor heating, a suspended bioethanol fireplace and rich textures making this place hard to leave – though if you do manage it there are bountiful adventures to be had nearby, from guided canoe trips and high-wire adventures to forest bathing and wild swimming in the River Wye. The Hudnalls books up months in advance, so plan ahead if you're hoping to flee for the trees.

The Hudnalls National Nature Reserve,
Loop Road, St Briavels, Lydney GL15 6SG
07986 168148
hudnallshideout.co.uk

The cabin includes all the ingredients you need to make use of the deck's pizza oven.

DESIGN The Hudnalls is significantly larger than most two-person hideaways. Vastness is a theme here, from the wraparound deck and picture windows to the woodland the tree-house exclusively inhabits. The Scandi decor fits in beautifully with the surroundings thanks to an abundance of wood and natural materials, though with a sense that no expense has been spared, from the floating fireplace down to the sheepskin throws that add tactility to every surface.

FACILITIES You're unlikely to want for much at The Hudnalls, which comes equipped with a stunning ensuite wet room and full kitchen complete with slimline dishwasher. On arrival, you'll discover a gorgeous assortment of welcome treats, including luxury toiletries to use in the outdoor bath and everything you need to make use of the deck's pizza oven.

LOCATION Escapes don't get more escapist than The Hudnalls, whose prime location on the edge of the Wye makes it the ultimate secluded stay. Spend it loafing on the sprawling deck or pack up some treats and head down to the private wildflower meadow for an al fresco feast (hamper and picnic blanket included).

NEARBY Thrill seekers and wellness enthusiasts are equally well catered for in the Wye Valley, with everything from stand-up paddleboarding and high-wire adventures to flotation therapy and foraging within easy reach. Alternatively, the local pub is just a 30-minute amble away.

With its outdoor copper tub, it's possible to bathe outdoors on the wraparound deck.

26

THE WATER CABIN

Minimalist retreat in the heart of the Norfolk Broads

Occupying a 1930s cedar-clad cabin on the banks of Norfolk's River Thurne, this tastefully restored hideaway makes a strong case for the soothing power of minimalist design. Neutrally decorated throughout with any fuss eschewed in favour of functional – but always beautiful – furnishings, the Water Cabin offers just what you need for a country escape. Positioned so close to the water you can sit on the deck and dangle your feet in, this stylish two-bedroom hideaway provides a stunning base from which to explore the Broads with family or friends, whether you choose to do it by paddleboard, kayak or even electric dayboat. Or, if that all sounds a bit too energetic for a relaxing retreat, simply watch the world (or swans) go by from that deck.

Water Cabin, Repps With Bastwick, Norfolk NR29
nor-folk.com

Situated on the banks of Norfolk's River Thurne, the cabin is ideally located for paddleboarding.

DESIGN To the untrained eye the Water Cabin might appear basic, but in fact it's been skilfully designed to create the most relaxing space possible, with high-end furnishings throughout. The cabin itself is highly energy-efficient and its windows are thoughtfully placed to generate the maximum amount of light. Natural browns, creams and greys lend warmth to the space, while subtle texture in the form of panelling, crinkled linens and dried grasses adds interest.

FACILITIES In the spirit of slow living, the Water Cabin doesn't have Wi-Fi, but there's still plenty to occupy you here, from a collection of inspirational travel and design books to a TV and DVD player for chilled film marathons. There's one twin and one double room, as well as a well-equipped kitchen and chic bathroom complete with a large walk-in shower, bath and products from the owners' vegan toiletries brand, Sop.

LOCATION Ideally located for paddleboarding (or however else you like to travel by water), the cabin enjoys a river frontage with a spacious deck and moorings. To the rear there's open countryside, with abundant walks, nature reserves and cycle routes to discover.

NEARBY As well as being the most complete medieval city in the UK, nearby Norwich boasts a thriving arts scene, and is home to a cornucopia of charming indie shops, restaurants and cafes. Alternatively, pack up your bucket and spade and head for the coastal towns of Great Yarmouth, Hemsby or Cromer, all less than an hours' drive away.

27

SETTLE

Handcrafted slow-living retreat in private parkland

Time seems to stand still at Settle, a whimsical hideaway set in 30 acres of tranquil private parkland in rural South Norfolk. The Lakeside Cabin, the luxurious jewel in Settle's crown, has been exquisitely crafted using salvaged materials and fittings from owners John and Jo Morfoot's reclamation yard, creating an extraordinarily restful space that epitomises the slow-living experience. There's lots to explore outside (albeit slowly and with intention), from the soulful lakes with their resident swans to the exceptionally well-curated on-site shops, Settle Store and Settle Shop, which offer fine groceries and artisanal lifestyle wares, respectively. Inside, it's just as breathtaking, with heritage timber-clad walls, a chic mix of Scandinavian and mid-century furniture and enormous vista-framing windows that summon in Mother Nature.

Larling Road, Shropham, Attleborough,
Norfolk NR17 1EA
01953 497030
settlenorfolk.co.uk

The lakeside bathhouse – separate from the main cabin – includes a wood-fired bathtub.

DESIGN The cabin's bespoke interiors are a lovingly assembled collage of salvaged materials, neutral hues and authentic textures. The craftmanship is astonishing, with every object beautifully made, restored or crafted, and the passionate attention to detail is palpable, from the abundant artisanal wares used throughout to the atmospheric artworks that hang on the walls.

FACILITIES Everything you could possibly require for a peaceful few days immersed in nature can be found in this stunning space, which feels more like a private residence than a holiday home. No expense has been spared on amenities, which include a freestanding stone egg bath with Meir tapware, a super-king bed with luxury linens and a stunning birch ply kitchen complete with heritage sink. Outside, guests can make use of their own deck-top pizza oven and log burner, but the real star of the show is the stunning lakeside bath house, which accommodates a wood-fired bath just a few steps from the cabin. You can even request a hamper loaded with sourdough bread, local butter, fresh coffee, oats, free-range eggs and fresh whole milk for outrageously decadent breakfasts in bed.

LOCATION Settle is located in the Breckland conservation area in Norfolk, a county known for its blue skies and low rainfall. As well as acres of private parkland to explore, guests can expect close encounters with wild muntjac, roe deer, hares, goats and chickens, as well as access to the two incredible on-site shops: Settle Store for fine groceries, including ready-to-cook pizzas, and Settle Shop for curated gifts to take home. The site is also home to three retired railway goods carriages, which have been sympathetically converted into luxurious lakeside havens, and two canvas safari tents for summertime glamping.

NEARBY It wouldn't be slow living if you were rushing about all over the place, and Settle is well-equipped for a stay spent purely on-site, with the thoughtfully stocked Settle Store negating the need for a supermarket run. If you do fancy venturing further afield, however, the lowlands of nearby Thetford and King's Forest, both a short drive away, offer miles of tranquil tracks to explore.

Settle Store, an on-site shop just a short walk from the cabin, offers beautifully made gifts to take home.

28

TURF HOUSE

Eccentric off-grid cabin with a Viking theme

This tiny retreat takes escapism to a whole new level, offering guests not only a chance to flee the grind (and the grid), but also to cosplay at being an actual Viking while they're there. Inspired by Iceland's Viking turf houses, this enchanting lodge is filled with references to Scandinavian seafaring folk, from horn drinking glasses to a Gjermundbu helmet (in case of unexpected invasions). That the Turf House is tiny is all part of the magic and doesn't stop it from being able to accommodate families, with rustic bunk beds included in addition to a cosy, faux-fur-lined double. Nestled between the spectacular Lake District and rugged Yorkshire Dales, it feels delightfully authentic, and after a few days of preparing rustic feasts on the barbecue, soaking in the old tin bath in front of the fire and exploring the unspoilt fells, you might begin to believe you've reached Valhalla.

Low Lane, Kirkby Stephen, Cumbria CA17 4NL
canopyandstars.co.uk

A turf roof completes the look of this earthy retreat, built using traditional ninth-century craftsmanship.

DESIGN Constructed using traditional methods employed since the ninth century, this off-grid lodge might look a glorified garden shed from the outside, all dry-stone walling and sheets of turf, but the interior is dramatically different, with beautifully handcrafted interiors, atmospheric oil lamps and a roaring fire creating an impossibly cosy vibe. The cabin's owners have excelled themselves in their quest to create a truly authentic Viking escape, right down to the wonky stools, hand-turned wooden crockery and hand-carved Drakkar figurines above the cabin door.

FACILITIES The complete lack of mod cons feels oddly welcome in this magical context (and yes, that includes the compost toilet and outdoor kitchen shack). Additional off-grid amenities include an ice-block cool box, a paraffin-heated shower for realistically lukewarm hose-downs, and a cast-iron teapot that you can heat on the stove, as well as a rather less historically accurate selection of books and board games for cosy evenings in.

LOCATION Perched on the northernmost tip of the Dales, at the borders of the Lakes and the Pennines, Bowber Head is one of the most beautifully wild spots in the UK, with access to virtually infinite walks on the doorstep.

NEARBY Kirkby Stephen's Fat Lamb is just a mile away and serves up a mouth-watering menu of locally sourced pub fare, while the historic market towns of Penrith and Kendal are just over 30 minutes' drive away – if you can bear to break character, that is.

29

TREES AT TUGHALL

Understated cabins with natural connection

With their wooden construction, ancient woodland location, and powerful connection with the ever-changing surroundings thanks to their huge view-framing windows, it's not hard to see why the owners of this handsome trio of cabins named them after trees. All identical – though with diverse views – and all following Tughall's guiding principle of distraction-free luxury, these two-person retreats offer everything you could need from a country escape and absolutely nothing you don't, being gloriously free from clutter both inside and out. Magnificently remote, located on a working farm an hour north of Newcastle-upon-Tyne on the edge of the Northumberland Coast Area of Outstanding Natural Beauty, the cabins Ash, Hawthorn and Willow all offer a superb base from which to explore England's northernmost county with its dramatic coastlines and magnificent fortresses.

Tughall Grange Farm, Chathill,
Northumberland NE67 5EN
07515053361
treesattughall.com

The cabin is only four fields along from Beadnell's stunning beach.

DESIGN Inspired by Scottish bothies and designed to interfere as little as possible with the surrounding landscape, the cabins feel like auditoriums for nature's never-ending theatre, all light wood panelling, natural linen and picture windows – complete with comfy window seats so you can get an even better look. Designed to be extensions of the outdoors as much as shelters from it, they all come complete with huge glass doors that open onto a decked patio, as well as a wood-burning stove and cosy throws for chillier days.

FACILITIES Each cabin offers a tiny but fully equipped black kitchen that's ideal for whipping up simple suppers. King-sized beds with memory-foam mattresses allow for luxurious lie-ins, while the beautifully angled, covered deck is perfect for al fresco loafing, whatever the weather.

LOCATION Tughall's idyllic location hits that sweet spot between totally secluded and easily accessible. Positioned four fields along from Beadnell village with its stunning horseshoe-shaped beach, and 30 minutes from the rolling Cheviot hills, it feels like the most unspoilt landscape on earth. If you're lucky, and very still, you might even spot Tughall's menagerie of swallows, hares, partridges, pheasants, roe deer and owls from the window, which functions as an incredible animal hide.

NEARBY Alnwick and Bamburgh castles are both within easy driving distance, whether you're in the mood for majestic gardens or an Anglo-Saxon fort. Gateshead is around an hour away, and home to both Antony Gormley's colossal *Angel of the North* sculpture and the superb Baltic Centre for Contemporary Art, while the town's neighbouring city of Newcastle-upon-Tyne is known for its nightlife.

30

THE CABLE HUT

Coastal hideaway with quirky past

Despite having been built to house telephone cables, this century-old Pembrokeshire dwelling couldn't feel more blissfully disconnected, set in a remote location at the top of a coastal track. Half traditional stone cottage, half corrugated iron hut, with a raised dual-aspect summerhouse at the rear of the site, this humble hideaway offers a breathtaking coastal vantage point whatever the season. A secluded hot tub and outdoor firepit with loungers on hand help you savour the summer months, and underfloor heating and a luxuriously deep bath keep you snug in winter. Well-suited to busy couples looking for a brief deceleration, this restful spot offers total stillness – the only exceptions being the tempestuous sea and the sun as it dramatically sets directly opposite the house (there's also cliff-diving and kayaking in case you really can't sit still).

Haverfordwest, Pembrokeshire SA62 5UX
+44 (0)1637 881183
uniquehomestays.com

Amble five minutes down the road to Aberbach Beach, home to seals and legends of local mermaids.

DESIGN Character is king at this history-seeped site, whose intriguing past is mirrored in its distinctive style. An antique cable-reel coffee table and original painted iron signage offer charming nods to the site's previous use, while pops of red keep it feeling contemporary. Designed to be as inviting in the colder months as in summer, the interior abounds with cosy home comforts, from a king-size cast-iron bed to a substantial velvet sofa, luxurious underfloor heating and Welsh wool textiles. Meanwhile, the summerhouse has more of a Scandinavian flavour, with wood panelling, stylish armchairs and minimalist decor that allows the wraparound views to sing, though still with an emphasis on comfort.

FACILITIES A modern fitted kitchen replete with dishwasher, washing machine, large fridge, Nespresso machine and full-sized oven allows for a civilised (and potentially lengthy) stay. The bathroom feels well equipped and luxurious, enjoying underfloor heating, a walk-in shower and a roll-top bath made for long soaks. Outside, a handful of terraced areas offer expansive views out to sea: choose from an elevated grassy area with sun loungers and a whimsical swing, a secluded patio area with a large hot tub and a table poised for lazy al fresco breakfasts, not forgetting the dreamy summerhouse at the top of the site (though it doesn't need to be summer for you to take full advantage) and an outdoor firepit for barbecues and marshmallow toasting.

LOCATION The Cable Hut occupies a spacious and deliciously remote site at the end of a discreet track, nestled between the coastal paths and endless fields behind. The property is a mere stone's throw from Aberbach Beach, a small pebble cove that reveals golden sand at low tide, with expansive views of the Irish Sea.

NEARBY Coastal walks begin on the doorstep, with secluded beaches within 400m. If you're seeking more of a buzz, there are copious opportunities for kayaking and cliff-jumping nearby. Or you can simply take a seat in the private garden and relish the melodramatic magnificence of the sea, keeping an eye out for the resident seabirds and marine mammals.

Enjoy the view from the wood-panelled summer house found at the rear of the site and set away from the main cabin.

Aberbach Beach, with its expansive views over the Irish Sea.

31

WATERFALL CABIN

Storybook sanctuary on the Welsh border

If it's full-on fairy tale magic you're after, head to this enchanting off-grid hideaway, whose setting is so idyllic you half expect a community of anthropomorphic mice to emerge from tiny doors in the trees. Positioned within the 1,000-acre Hafod Estate, this filmic stilted cabin offers everything you could possibly need for a romantic getaway, with a wood-fired outdoor hot tub, inviting hayloft bed and a suspended stargazing net where you can make like the Welsh and *cwtch* (that's cuddle) under a twinkling sky. All stays last for three or four nights, giving you ample time to sample the local pottery's throwing lessons, the nearby pubs and spectacular hikes around the estate, though if you'd prefer to spend the duration enjoying a lack of obligations, phone signal and other humans... well, it's perfect for that too.

Near Pont-rhyd-y-groes, Ceredigion SY25
kiphideaways.com

DESIGN Perfectly designed to make the most of the surrounding forest, Waterfall Cabin rises gracefully above a grassy glen, with bifold doors that open up the living space and a spacious veranda supported by wooden stilts. Everything here has been carefully considered, from the bespoke wooden kitchenette to the expertly chosen antiques and locally crafted ceramics, with almost nothing that is not both useful and beautiful.

FACILITIES Owners Pip and Lee have thought of everything. There is a wheelbarrow to transport your belongings from car to cabin; clear, practical instructions and maps; and thoughtful extras including a well-curated library and even art supplies – just in case the beautiful surroundings inspire creativity. All amenities are completely off-grid, with a gas hob for cooking, an ice-box chiller, a self-contained compostable toilet (in a separate hut) and a battery-powered camping shower. Outside, a swing seat, hot tub, hammock and rustic seating area complete with a firepit (plus cookware) help guests maximise their time spent in nature.

LOCATION Nestled in the picturesque Cambrian Mountains, the Hafod Estate is home to miniature waterfalls, brooks and meandering forest footpaths. The cabin itself occupies a secluded yet sunny spot among the trees that takes your breath away as it comes into view at the bottom of the path, and is regularly visited by swooping red kites, otters and hares.

NEARBY The Y Ffarmers country gastropub is a 25-minute drive from the cabin in the village of Llanfihangel-y-Creuddyn – just seven miles from Aberystwyth. You're also offered the opportunity to take part in a Red Kite-feeding experience, or even try your hand at throwing with a personal pottery class from local tutors David and Anouska at Penrhiw Pottery, whose stunning stoneware can be found throughout the cabin.

The wood-fired hot tub is a cosy touch for the colder months.

32

HERGEST LEE

Custom-designed cabin with room for children

If you're a parent, you might think that bringing your kids with you negates the purpose of a relaxing rural retreat, but this delightful cabin is too perfect to not at least consider dragging the little ones along. Custom-built by owner Paul Gent, this cedar-framed lodge boasts a softly curved roof that elegantly mirrors the undulations of the adjacent hillside, as well as allowing room for a cosy mezzanine sleep space perfectly suited to young children. Don't worry if kids aren't in the picture, though. Abundant opportunities for canoeing, horse riding, wild swimming and nearby walks make it just as perfect for wildlife-loving couples and outdoor sports fans. Or, if you just fancy detoxing from reality with a long soak and cosy night's sleep in a lovingly crafted, mid-century modern hideaway bounded by spectacular scenery (and let's face it, who doesn't?), this Welsh belle is for you.

Burlingjobb, Powys LD8
07920181000
hergest-lee.com

Hergest Lee's architecture is designed to mirror the curves of the nearby Hanter Hill.

DESIGN Almost as breath-taking as the valleys that surround it, this thoughtfully designed hideaway feels both luxurious and functional, with decadent elements including a squashy leather sofa and Victorian clawfoot bath employed alongside bespoke modular furniture that can be neatly slotted away when not in use. Handmade from durable cedar, the kitchen and bedroom units create a sense of continuity along with the floating staircase, while well-chosen antique finds add character and a thoughtful mix of wood, leather, wool and linen creates texture. The resulting aesthetic is seriously sophisticated – think mid-century modern meets Scandi cabin in the woods – but still very liveable, even with kids in tow.

FACILITIES This place has it all, from luxury inclusions such as Bang & Olufsen speakers, Piglet in Bed linen and a roll-top bath, to an extendable kitchen table and extra sleep space that make it ideal for families (the extra bed is in the eaves and has a very low ceiling, so is only really suitable for small children). As well as a fully equipped kitchen there's an outdoor firepit and grill, allowing for al fresco feasts in dry weather, as well as a shower and complimentary toiletries. Guests can also help themselves to board games and a small library of books, and a TV is available on request.

LOCATION Private without feeling remote, the cabin is located in the scenic heart of rural Wales, close to the border with Herefordshire, and enjoys an elevated position overlooking the magnificent Hergest Ridge and Hanter Hill. Close to other buildings but not overlooked, the cabin includes its own private garden with lavender and wildflowers, as well as a firepit and a bistro table set.

NEARBY As well as being close to many wild swimming spots, the cabin is perfectly placed for plentiful scenic walks, including one leading to the local Harp Inn, a family-owned longhouse with ancient slate floors, oak beams, a log fire and expansive views across the landscape. The world-renowned literary town of Hay-on-Wye is just a short drive away and hosts an annual book festival as well as dozens of bookshops.

The cabin is well-located for nearby wild swimming, with Powys home to some of the best spots in the UK.

CABINS

33

FFOREST FARM

Community-focused site that's great for groups

Rural retreats aren't always about holding hands in hammocks and hot tubs built for two. Fforest Farm's rustic shacks promote community over coupledom, sleeping groups of up to six and being part of a small village-like site comprising a range of accommodation, a communal lodge where guests can grab their morning granola, a cedar-barrel sauna and even an adorable one-room pub with its own resident ghost. Set within a 200-acre site next to the Teifi marshes nature reserve, the Fforest shacks have been conceived as somewhere to enjoy the simplicity of outdoor living in a spectacular natural environment, with plenty to do on site and delightfully comfortable cabins to come back to. Ideal for outdoorsy families or groups of friends – and a great place to make new ones.

Cwm Plysgog, Cardigan, Cilgerran,
Pembrokeshire SA43 2TB
+44 (0)1239 800200
coldatnight.co.uk

DESIGN Each of Fforest's three garden shacks comprises one twin and two double bedrooms, all with their own desk area, as well as snug Welsh blankets and cosy cushions. Outside, a covered rustic private kitchen, dining area with vintage table with chapel chairs and an L-shaped sofa overlook raised beds bursting with wildflowers, herbs and seasonal vegetables. Pine panelling provides insulation, keeping the cabin cool in the summer months and snug in the winter.

FACILITIES While there are no bathroom facilities inside the cabins, the outdoor showers and toilet block (one shower and one toilet for each cabin) are just a few steps away. Just up the path from the shacks, the welcoming Lodge serves a delicious breakfast of homemade granola, local jams, freshly baked bread and proper coffee, which can be savoured while gazing out across the surrounding meadows.

LOCATION Situated by the River Teifi gorge, minutes from the town of Cardigan and the beautiful beaches and coves of the west Wales coast, this vast and blissful site offers a variety of accommodation, from unique geodesic domes to a huge Georgian farmhouse and luxurious crog lofts. As well as the communal lodge, guests are welcome to make use of a soothing cedar-barrel sauna hidden just inside the woods, or enjoy a tipple at Y Bwthyn, an inviting (though haunted) one-room pub that's converted from an old stone cottage and boasts a full bar, countless candles and roaring open fireplace.

NEARBY Pizzatipi's mouth-watering potato pizza makes a visit to this Cardigan institution – a ten-minute drive or 40-minute walk away – a must. Head to nearby villages such as St Dogmaels or Cilgerran for cute cafes and antique shops. Fforest is also close to many of Wales's most picturesque beaches, including the popular Mwnt Beach, the pristine, dune-backed Poppit Sands and Tresaith Beach with its ample rock pools and impressive cliffside waterfall.

The garden shacks overlook the raised bed garden, full of seasonal vegetables, herbs and wildflowers.

34

EAGLE BRAE

Classic log cabins in a theatrical Highland setting

Contemplating a Highland fling? This handsome collection of ten rustic log cabins is perfectly placed for an authentic Scottish getaway, immersed in 8,000 acres of rugged scenery close to both Inverness and Loch Ness and with traditional designs that are crafted entirely by hand – down to their chunky tree-trunk frames. Cabins sleep two to six guests, making them as great for couples' retreats as they are family holidays or mates' escapes, but the capacious Loxia, Aquila and Buteo cabins are particularly suited to groups (boasting mezzanine log beds that are ideal for kids), as well as a peaceful pond-side location. In addition to daily visits from the resident deer, guests can expect surround-sound birdsong and cinematic scenery, with bountiful on-site outdoor pursuits to choose from. The real McCoy of Highland holidays – kilt optional.

Eagle Brae, Struy IV4 7LE
01463 761301
eaglebrae.co.uk

The cabins' cosy interiors are hand-sawed and chiselled from Western red cedar.

DESIGN Each of Eagle Brae's quintessentially Scottish cabins has been lovingly hand-sawed and chiselled from Western red cedar to create a rugged-luxe aesthetic of which Braveheart would approve. Sustainably designed to exude cosy comfort in all seasons, the charismatic hideaways feature green wildflower roofs and biomass-fuelled underfloor heating, with natural interiors that blend effortlessly with the surroundings (think hand-carved panels, tartan textiles and dramatic antler chandeliers).

FACILITIES The cabins' hosts love to pamper their guests and every party receives a large welcome hamper stuffed with fine Scottish products on arrival. The larger cabins all come with full-sized family kitchens comprising a washing machine, dishwasher and everything else you could need, with the whole site powered by on-site renewables via a micro-hydro scheme. Toiletries, laundry products, a PC with printer and even a bird feeder are just a few of the ample amenities you can enjoy. Literally all you need to bring are your holiday-ready selves.

LOCATION Eagle Brae is only a 20-mile drive from Inverness and yet it still manages to feel like the ends of the earth. Nestled between the magical Glen Affric – often described as the most beautiful glen in Scotland – and the remote Glen Strathfarrar, this 8,000-acre site is an epic patchwork of shady woodland, clear lakes and endless valleys, where wildlife roams free. There are ten cabins in total but they're scattered evenly across the site, so you're still more likely to bump into a deer than another human.

NEARBY With so much to do on-site and in the surrounding area, you won't have much chance to get bored here – that is, unless you really want to be. Clay pigeon shooting, canoeing, pony trekking and even dog sledding are all available on the doorstep, while the delights of idyllic Beauly – home to the historic Beauly Priory – and the enigmatic Loch Ness are just a short drive away.

Deer roam free on this 8,000-acre site nestled between Glen Affric and Glen Strathfarrar.

35

HARLOSH

Luxurious minimalist hideaway in spectacular landscape

If you like your getaways with a liberal serving of drama, then this striking Hebridean cabin is for you. Understated yet sumptuous, and with an eye-catchingly boxy silhouette that seems to simultaneously clash and blend in with Skye's breathtakingly rugged scenery, it's the perfect spot from which to experience this extraordinary island, whether you're braving the elements or hunkering down to enjoy them from the comfort of the Scandi-style interior. Ideal for couples' getaways, the cabin comes complete with everything you could desire for a romantic week in the wilderness, and with top-rated restaurants, distilleries and once-in-a-lifetime outdoor pursuits all right on the doorstep. A getaway in the deepest sense of the word.

Ardmore, Dunvegan, Isle of Skye IV55 8ZJ
harlosh.co

This striking black-clad cabin feels at home in Skye's dramatic surroundings.

DESIGN Fans of minimalist design will feel effortlessly at home at this tasteful black-clad cabin, whose restful interior combines dove-grey cement flooring, neutral-toned textiles and clean white walls to striking – but never austere – effect. In the true spirit of minimalism, everything serves a purpose, and every detail has been meticulously considered, from the impeccably chosen furniture to the floor-to-ceiling windows that transform every room into a theatre from which to observe the magnificent vistas.

FACILITIES The decor might be understated, but there's no skimping on amenities at Harlosh. From the well-equipped kitchen to a smart TV with soundbar for rainy days, the space has been designed with modern life in mind, and you could easily spend ten days here before you start craving civilisation. Even the fundamentals feel impossibly luxurious: think stunning mid-century-style sofa, king-sized bed with deluxe bedding and sheepskin-draped armchairs for lounging.

LOCATION Situated on the west coast of Skye, Harlosh offers an escape like no other, with diverse wildlife including birds of prey, deer, otters and dolphins, and spectacular scenery that will make you feel as though you've journeyed to the very edge of the earth.

NEARBY Foodies will rejoice at the excellent choice of restaurants in the area, including the world-renowned Three Chimneys, vegetarian spot Chidakasha and The Dunvegan, where food made with locally sourced Scottish ingredients is cooked over fire. Skye's Talisker Distillery is only half an hour by car, afterwards pop into the neighbouring Caora Dhubh Coffee Company for a slice of cake to soak up the whiskey. The magical Fairy Pools are around an hour's drive away, and the fascinating Dunvegan Castle is just 15 minutes. On perfectly still nights, you might even manage to catch a glimpse of the northern lights from your doorstep.

HIDDEN
SCOTLAND
03.

The cabin is a short drive from Talisker Distillery where it is possible to sample traditional local whiskey.

36

THE LODGE DUN ALUINN

Lavish cottage that's great for groups

The words 'caretaker's bungalow' may not immediately conjure images of wanton luxury, but this capacious lodge has undergone quite the transformation since its days as a staff residence, even picking up multiple architectural awards along the way. Today, this former 1950s prefab offers an extraordinary country escape for groups of up to eight people, set within five-and-a-half acres of private parkland close to the picturesque town of Aberfeldy, with jaw-dropping panoramas over the River Tay. A wonderful backdrop for special celebrations and long overdue get-togethers, the lodge incorporates four ensuite bedrooms and ample communal living space, including a calm and cosy lounge with a spectacular feature fireplace, and a vast, stage-like deck that's ideal for outdoor entertaining. Got a bigger group to entertain? The adjacent main house at Dun Aluinn can be hired concurrently for even grander gatherings.

Alma Avenue, Aberfeldy PH15 2BW
07850 857550
dunaluinn.com

DESIGN The Lodge's exterior is loosely based on North American log cabins, but the setting is unmistakably Scottish, with its moody skies and lush carpet of purple wildflowers in the grounds. Its many interior inspirations include Stanley Kubrick's cinematic masterpiece, *2001: A Space Odyssey*, with swathes of white lifted by the occasional pop of colour – usually in the form of a cushion or a bespoke wash basin. Indeed, it's all about the little details at Dun Aluinn, whose mid-century Scandi decor comes exquisitely to life through beautifully chosen objects and artworks by local artists.

FACILITIES The open-plan kitchen comes equipped with world-class cooking facilities and ample preparation surfaces, though you can also arrange on-site catering and housekeeping services if you want to completely unwind.

LOCATION The Lodge is situated within walking distance of Aberfeldy and a 90-minute drive from both Edinburgh and Glasgow airports, making it feel easily accessible in spite of its remote location. Though part of the Dun Aluinn estate, the property benefits from its own private entrance and grounds, as well as a large, decked area complete with firepit and stylish outdoor seating, including a swing chair imported from Ibiza.

NEARBY The sleepy town of Aberfeldy is just 600 metres from the estate, with plenty of cute bookshops and interiors boutiques to peruse, and several excellent coffee spots and restaurants. As well as being within easy reach of many amazing walks and mountain-biking trails, guests are well-placed to take advantage of a variety of bespoke Highland experiences, from guided walks and safaris to white-water rafting and canyoning. Birks, a local Art Deco community cinema, is also a short walk away.

ARAN

37

BLUE HARE

Modernist hideaway on an otherworldly island

If modern life has you contemplating a move to the moon, try an out-of-this-world escape to this asymmetrical cabin first. Like a marooned spacecraft wedged between the craters, this mesmerising hideout is as unique as the magical landscape that surrounds it, its angular structure and grey cladding blending beautifully into the craggy coastal scenery. Perfectly placed windows and thoughtful details, including a pair of sea-facing armchairs, make Blue Hare an incredible spot from which to admire Harris's ever-changing skies. Such an awe-inspiring setting, however, deserves to be explored properly, be it kayaking in the adjacent cove, taking on one of the island's numerous hiking trails or relaxing on one of its picture-perfect beaches, where white sand meets turquoise waves. Head here in late September or October for a chance to catch the northern lights and an even greater sense of having journeyed beyond the earth.

19b Lingerbay, Isle of Harris HS3 3JE
07831 390216
bluehare.scot

DESIGN The cabin's hard-edged shell conceals a warm, comfy interior characterised by elegant wood panels, soft colours and a sense of stylish practicality. Small but perfectly formed, the open-plan living and sleeping space offers a calm and cosy haven for two. Well-placed floor-to-ceiling windows optimise your enjoyment of the incredible location, whether you're marvelling at the starlit skies from the perfectly positioned armchairs or enjoying one of the most incredible showers of your life in the terrazzo-tiled wet room.

FACILITIES Blue Hare comes equipped with everything guests could need for a relaxing stay in a compact space, including a full kitchen with a washing machine, fridge, oven, dining table and dishwasher, as well as a welcoming wood burner and wall-mounted TV for cosy evenings in. The rainforest shower will make you feel at one with nature while you're washing (even if the luxurious underfloor heating shatters the illusion somewhat). Outside, enjoy lazy barbecues and sunset dining on the sizeable deck.

LOCATION Perched on a rugged hillside at the southern end of magical Harris, this remarkable hideaway enjoys arresting sea views on one side and snow-capped mountain scenes on the other. The seemingly endless, turbulent skies appear to change before your eyes, transforming from tangerine sunsets to eerie fog and star-scattered wonder at night. With scenery that feels closer to Norway than Scotland, this outdoor lovers' favourite provides all the respite of a foreign holiday without the need for a passport.

NEARBY The views from the cabin might be stunning, but fully immersing yourself in the scenery is something else entirely – there are numerous secluded coves and not-so-well-trodden hiking trails on the doorstep, and plenty of marine wildlife to spot on the coast. Adventure seekers should head to nearby Lingerbay Loch, where outdoor activities span fishing, swimming, paddleboarding and kayaking, while those craving more of a buzz will find countless surfing opportunities in the bracing waters of the Hebrides.

38

57 NORD

Minimalist luxury in stunning surroundings

Picture your typical cabin, and Danish designer lighting and sommelier-selected wine probably aren't the first things that spring to mind – but then 57 Nord's Hill House isn't your typical cabin. Overlooking the meeting point of three ancient sea lochs and the medieval Eilean Donan Castle, this unique hideaway offers a magical guest experience that aligns with its fairy tale setting, with luxurious interiors inspired by the region's Scandi-Gaelic heritage and windows revealing views so exquisite they resemble vast landscape paintings. Ideal for groups, this two-bedroom cabin has all the indulgent appeal of a high-end spa, with its minimalist decor and the owner's insistence on providing the finest version of everything, from the bathtub to the toiletries, not to mention the contents of the wonderful welcome hamper that greets you on arrival. A true sanctuary for self-care and slow living – even if it only lasts a few glorious days.

57 Nord Upper Ardelve, Ross-Shire IV40 8EY
57nord.co.uk

DESIGN With its opulent mix of minimalist Scandi style, mid-century design and fine Scottish craftsmanship, 57 Nord's Hill House feels more like a boutique hotel than a cabin, though with all the secluded calm of the latter. Designed to tie in with the landscape, the tranquil interiors make extensive use of natural, locally produced materials. Highlights include a deep stone bathtub resembling a giant pebble, contemporary Scottish textiles and sculptural Danish-designed lighting throughout.

FACILITIES The cabin has been kitted out with every high-end appliance, product and fitting you could wish for, from products by cult Swedish beauty brand L:A Bruket in the bathrooms to ceramics handmade by Edinburgh-based Borja Moronta and a hamper stuffed with artisanal food and drink. The fully stocked, sommelier-curated wine fridge comes complete with tasting notes, while the award-winning, locally roasted, single-origin coffee includes a detailed brewing guide. The huge windows with their ever-changing views are infinitely better than a TV, but there is one included anyway in case you want cuddle up with your favourite programme by the log burner.

LOCATION Surrounded by breathtaking natural wonders, Hill House occupies an incredible position on the edge of Wester Ross in the craggy Scottish Highlands, resulting in some of the most magical views you'll likely ever experience. Reassuringly private, the expansive outdoor space includes a yoga-ready deck (and some seating, in case you're feeling slightly less energetic).

NEARBY All guests receive a copy of the cabin's beautifully compiled in-house guide, which comes stuffed with recommendations for the area's best restaurants, artisans, distilleries and walks, along with suggested itineraries. Private tours and boat trips can be arranged with the owner on request, and fresh, juicy langoustines can be purchased daily from the local fisherman – just a five-minute walk away.

One of 57 Nord's two cabins (the other being Sky House), Hill House's stunning location offers incredible views.

A view of the meeting point of three lochs, with the medieval Eilean Donan Castle on the left.

British Cabins and Hideaways: An Opinionated Guide
First edition, first printing

Published in 2023 by Hoxton Mini Press, London

Text and photography by Holly Farrier*
Edited by Emmy Watts
Copy-edited by Florence Ward
Series design by Hoxton Mini Press
Production design by Richard Mason
Cover and map illustration by Charlotte Ager
Editorial support by Megan Baffoe

Holly would like to thank her parents Shayne and Becky, as well as David and Helena for their invaluable support. To everyone who accompanied me on cabin trips, thank you for making this experience so special: Ollie, Vesper, David, Jenny, Dan, Talulah and Becky. Dan, thank you for everything, this book wouldn't be what it is without you.

*Except for following images: Aurora and Firefly (all images) ©Unique Homestays www.uniquehomestays.com; Lodge at Dun Aluinn (all images) courtesy of Dun Aluinn, (first and last images) by Ruth Maria Murphy, (all other images) by Fran Matt; Tree's at Tughall (all images) courtesy of Olco Studios and KOTO; Turf House (all images) courtesy of Canopy & Stars.

A CIP catalogue record for this book is available from the British Library.

ISBN: 978-1-914314-52-0

Printed and bound by OZGraf, Poland

Hoxton Mini Press is an environmentally conscious publisher, committed to offsetting our carbon footprint. This book is 100 per cent carbon compensated, with offset purchased from Stand For Trees.

For every book you buy from our website, we plant a tree:
www.hoxtonminipress.com